SOURCE BOOKS IN ARCHITECTURE

TATIANA BILBAO ESTUDIO

SOURCE BOOKS IN ARCHITECTURE | KNOWLTON SCHOOL | THE OHIO STATE UNIVERSITY | BENJAMIN WILKE, SERIES EDITOR

16 TATIANA BILBAO ESTUDIO

APPLIED RESEARCH +DESIGN

Published by Applied Research and Design Publishing, an imprint of ORO Editions.
Gordon Goff: Publisher

www.appliedresearchanddesign.com
info@appliedresearchanddesign.com

Contributors: Tatiana Bilbao, Kay Bea Jones, Deborah Berke, Benjamin Wilke
Book Design: Benjamin Wilke
Editor: Benjamin Wilke
Design & Editorial Assistance: Andi Moore
Project Manager: Jake Anderson

10 9 8 7 6 5 4 3 2 1 First Edition

ISBN: 978-1-961856-06-6

Color Separations and Printing: ORO Editions Inc.
Printed in China.

AR+D Publishing makes a continuous effort to minimize the overall carbon footprint of its publications. As part of this goal, AR+D, in association with Global ReLeaf, arranges to plant trees to replace those used in the manufacturing of the paper produced for its books. Global ReLeaf is an international campaign run by American Forests, one of the world's oldest nonprofit conservation organizations. Global ReLeaf is American Forests' education and action program that helps individuals, organizations, agencies, and corporations improve the local and global environment by planting and caring for trees.

CONTENTS

Collegium pigmented concrete model

Pilgrim's Route Gratitude Open Chapel collage

INTRODUCTION

DEBORAH BERKE

Tatiana Bilbao is one of the most exciting architects working today. It gives me great pleasure to write that sentence as I think of her work as exciting not because it is flamboyant (it is not), luxurious (it is decidedly not), or self-important (it would never be), but because it calls out to everyone who experiences it exactly what architecture can do.

Tatiana Bilbao founded her practice Tatiana Bilbao ESTUDIO in 2004 in Mexico City, where she is currently based. While much of her work is centered in Mexico City and across Mexico, she also has projects around the world. Wherever she builds, shapes comprehensive plans, assembles collaborative design teams, or creates housing and public spaces, the work is driven by her strong principles of social good. She designs buildings for people and through them creates spaces for communities. She actively resists gentrification, emphasizing affordability. She equally actively supports education, culture, and housing for all.

While at Ohio State, Tatiana covered aspects of practicing architecture with a guiding philosophy, meaning, and direction. She did this through discussions around the broad scope of her projects and built works. This is very much her nature and approach. In this volume you will find four projects covered in detail: Lyon La Confluence; Housing+ in Acuña; Olive West in St. Louis, Missouri; and the Kloster Maria Friedenshort.

At Lyon La Confluence, she was responsible for three buildings that each provided housing—social housing in two, and market-rate in the third. They are sober yet sensuous structures, deeply sensitive to indoor-outdoor interactions and to natural light. Housing+ is an affordable housing design, conceived for several locations in Mexico. The project's realization in Acuña helped address the needs of a community impacted by a tornado in 2015. Funded in part by Mexico's federal housing agency, the structures are ecologically sensitive and filled with life. The project is shaped by respect for its inhabitants along with a clear understanding of how the interrelated nature of extended families is interwoven into the creation and identity of place. She brings this same sensitivity at Olive West, a dense comprehensive plan for housing in a neglected area of the city. Emily Rauh Pulitzer, philanthropist and founder of the Pulitzer Arts Foundation, initiated the project as an attempt to understand appropriate forms of housing for the twenty-first century in a city that has seen both the creation of wealth and significant decay. The shared outdoor spaces in the design proposal will provide this renewed neighborhood with a park that knits the community together. While religious communities and urban neighborhoods do not typically have a lot in common, Bilbao's proposed Neuzelle Monastery building for Cistercian monks outside Brandenburg, Germany will do the same for their self-created community by offering opportunities for intimacy, privacy, and reflection alongside spaces for collective celebration and work.

This is the work of an architect committed to bettering the lives of those who live in, work in, and study in or experience her buildings and spaces. Sharing this with students offers them the inspiration, I hope, to find their version of this approach to practice as well.

Tatiana has become my friend, but I met her initially at the Yale School of Architecture when she was invited to be the Louis I. Kahn Visiting Assistant Professor of Architecture, a position created to bring young talent to teach at the school. When I became Dean, I invited her to return to Yale, where she is currently the Charles Gwathmey Professor in Practice, a multi-year appointment that allows her to deeply investigate—through research-based advanced design studios—issues of domesticity.

Her teaching work, like all her work, has been awe-inspiring and joyous. She shows us that it is possible to be serious about one's goals without losing the joy of creativity.

On the wall of my studio at home hangs a collage by Tatiana, a gift following a particularly meaningful semester of teaching. It shows a portal, undeniably domestic, speaking to promise and the path ahead. It has the light of the sun, the definition of walls, and the presence of greenery. I look at it as I draw, and I smile at the strength of the convictions that contribute to the impact of her work.

THE CULTURE OF CARE AND COLLABORATION: Teaching with Tatiana Bilbao

KAY BEA JONES

On a temperate late October evening, the final year students at the Ohio State Knowlton School of Architecture Master's Program had assembled at my home prepared to meet Tatiana Bilbao for the first time. This year's iteration of the KSA Baumer Seminar taught each autumn semester had been evolving weekly since August. The course is a requirement for the graduating master class in architecture. Typically, the objective of this course is to instruct advanced students with lessons most readily accessible through direct contact with a reflective practitioner to glean deep insights from selected buildings by that renowned designer.

The current group of thirty-one students had been scrutinizing Tatiana Bilbao ESTUDIO's built work along with the architect's proposals, exhibitions, ideas, and lectures. They had accessed Bilbao's intentions through close readings of foundational texts of theory that she and I had assigned to them. The students had been formulating their questions for her for several weeks. On this social occasion they were anticipating with great enthusiasm their first face-to-face contact with her, and they found it difficult holding off on the edible spread that awaited them. Tatiana's flight had arrived hours ago, albeit delayed, and she had notified us that she was on her way. The excitement was building. So was the hunger.

Finally with the sun getting low we saw the architect rounding the corner hand in hand with her nine-year-old daughter, Alessa. They moved slowly. Alessa was bending frequently. It had taken them twenty minutes to walk a block and a half because the girl was collecting all the colored oak and maple leaves from the sidewalk as they ambled through my residential neighborhood. She doesn't have fall foliage at home in Mexico City, Tatiana said, and it was her first experience of autumn in Ohio. Alessa, it turns out, is a precocious, observant, well-traveled kid.

The Culture of Care

Why is the notion of the "care city" relevant to this exposé? For Bilbao, the post-pandemic sustainable city is the "City of Care." The personal dwelling is the dominant structure and the centerpiece of her architectural problematic, and she has spent decades surveying deficits in modern urban equality with a particular focus on her country's inability to provide sufficient, affordable housing in the postwar era despite Mexico's constitutional mandate. Historically, as well as currently, the home is considered a refuge from work and the outside world. It is to be the place of comfort and rest. Yet it has rarely been exclusively or expressly so for most primary caregivers. Those tasked by gender or social contracts who bear the burdens of caring for others have long known that the virtues of home are relative, and as their place of work, finding repose in its spaces is a fraught exercise. Each generation has modeled a form of typical residence that asserts its timeliness, its "modernity," yet rarely are our presumptions challenged about the forms of public and private domains that assign some of its dwellers to servitude. The kitchen is a perpetual food factory; laundry and cleaning represent endless, repetitive tasks; and these workloads are often invisible since they are not valued in our commodity-driven culture. We monetize all resources but do not recognize all forms of labor. While salaries bind workers in a class structure, unsalaried work is overlooked, taken for granted, and indeterminately valued, if it is valued at all. The implications for the design of housing and the home, especially where shortages are ubiquitous, is paramount to fomenting residential design research in the current academy where experimental practices for architecture can emerge. Bilbao's recent exhibitions, unbuilt experimental models, and built dwellings provide ample testimony. She calls for reconsideration of the centrality of care in the house that serves as a home in both her pedagogy and her design practice.

The magnitude of family care responsibilities for an architect with a global practice and international teaching career have significant implications, especially where insufficient childcare persists. Tatiana readily acknowledges that she is privileged to have childcare options, and her focus on the care economy is more academic than experiential. Yet the pandemic taught her the insufficiency of most private dwelling environments, including her own, to adapt to meet the needs of collective care when it becomes necessary. Engaging her daughter, Alessa, while teaching abroad provided my students with the opportunity to consider some alternatives to traditional work rituals. The problem of inequitable labor and social expectations that rely on determined patterns and typologies for the home has captured Bilbao's imagination to inform her critique of modern housing and its economies. Her introspective models and installations in international exhibitions have stimulated her and others' design activism.

Bilbao has long addressed the problem of scale in the realm of need-based housing in Mexico. We learn on the website for Tatiana Bilbao ESTUDIO: "Tatiana Bilbao began her eponymous studio in 2004 with the aim of integrating social values, collaboration, and sensitive design approaches to architectural work. Prior to founding her firm, Bilbao was an Advisor in the Ministry of Development and Housing of the Government of the Federal District of Mexico City. During this period, she was part of the General Development Directorate of the Advisory Council for Urban Development in the City."[1] As she writes about her story, however, we find that her targeted criticism of the status quo was not readily embraced by her government, and her leadership has been hard won requiring coordination among like-hearted architects. As she gathered a cohort of colleagues to establish a collective voice, she and her allies have spoken out with informed determination and dissent.

American Dream for Sale

The Mexican Constitution of 1917 includes a provision for housing as a universal human right. In practice, we learn that the fourty-three square meters to which every Mexican citizen is entitled has resulted in a complex history of incomplete and unsatisfactory communities. The struggle has galvanized Bilbao's professional efforts. In her 2018 book *A House Is Not Just a House: Projects on Housing*, from the Columbia University series on books about architecture and the city, she itemizes the modern history of Mexican housing that began with expansion around the edges of the capital city and across the nation. Trending privatization eventually called for her dedication to improve government sponsored mass housing while questioning the value systems driving its design.

Bilbao traces the postwar patterns of popular housing by architects including Mario Pani and José María Gutiérrez Trujillo that resulted in relatively successful communities for their era that were well suited to their constituents. Most notable is the fact that these structures continue today to be inhabited as both social and market-rate housing. Bilbao's description of early walkable settlements evokes images of American prewar greenbelt models in which architects designed public environments with a wide variety of unit types and ranges of sizes that supported collective living. She attributes the desirability of the featured 1940s and 1950s models surrounding Mexico City in part to their circumstantial location. These neighborhoods have since been absorbed into the city that has sprawled beyond them. Variability in multifamily housing designs meant that different family sizes were supported. Collaborative financing and construction, especially when factory owners were involved, brought shared land holdings and investments in cultural and social programing. Modern construction was not perfect, but experimentation with materials produced dynamic expressions that distinguished the resulting works of architecture. Rapid growth around these new neighborhoods saw the city expand to envelop them. Government financing and construction models restrained profits. Urban infrastructure including roads, transit, schools, churches, and social and commercial centers fostered community continuity and a relatively good quality of life.

The last government-commissioned housing was built in the region in 1972. During the 1980s disasters such as the 1985 earthquake led to explosive needs for shelter, which in turn brought privatization and market-driven projects built with large-scale speculative investments. Exponential growth in demand brought the end of the *ejido*, the traditional communal ownership of land. Struck down by President Salinas de Gortari in 1992, the privatization of lands has caused massive housing growth with enormous profits to independent developers who invested only in single-family units causing a radical departure from the previous diversified social models.[2] In addition, the developer spreadsheet drove the purchase of inexpensive new lands located far from the city that did not have the necessary infrastructure to link the working poor to jobs, health care, schools, and markets. Under President Vincente Fox, who was elected in 2000, 2.5 million houses were constructed by private investors over six years.[3]

Bilbao has called out the detrimental effects of the transition from social to private market housing and identified it as an appropriation of the Levittown car-centric model of American home ownership. In her critique, she recognizes independence as an unwarranted premium of the model that was infinitely seductive and addictive. The movement was fostered by attempts to "sell the story of the little dream houses" whose pitched roofs, gardens, and parking were symbolic of the perfect family. Yet such privatized social housing was soon to fail.[4] Nearly upon completion many recently built mega-scale neighborhoods in isolation became a planning nightmare. Mortgages went unpaid, developers lost money, the government held bad credit, and units were nearly 30 percent abandoned. Bilbao approached INFONAVIT, the federally owned bank that grants loans to fund the construction of massive housing developments, to point out the causes of these failures. At the time they were unwilling to hear her criticisms. So instead, she organized other architects to study the problem and to understand together causal issues while seeking solutions that would better address what people most wanted and needed. In the process, these coalitions discovered their political agency, even while establishing unexpected alliances with political agencies.

Bilbao was later hired by SEDESOL, the Mexican government's development department, to join a team already designing a 600-unit complex for families displaced by a mudslide in Michoacán. Tatiana Bilbao ESTUDIO was able to begin with the comprehensive site plan and was asked to collaborate with a local architect already working on site. Lessons from this project focused on the importance of the identity of long-time dwellers in the town and the need for flexibility and expansion of the singular unit. Designers responded to the needs of residents and to the local topography to provide unit types that have gained value, because their residents indeed value them. Initial units provided for essential functions while opportunities to expand these dwellings provided flexibility as families grow. Further reflection on the amended process has led Bilbao to question the market value model toward better understanding the human values for the primary dwellers they aim to serve.[5]

Bilbao's experience working on La Confluence in Lyon, France, as a design team member for the urban housing development planned by Herzog and De Meuron afforded her a new appreciation for the economics of building in Mexico. She has noted that in France 25 percent of new dwelling structures are federally sponsored projects in the form of integrated social housing that provide for the unemployed, unlike in Mexico where residents must have jobs to be eligible for sponsored homes. The French government's efforts to meet social objectives is ambitious notwithstanding significantly higher costs of construction.

In Lyon, Bilbao was commissioned to design three residential towers within Herzog and De Meuron's urban plan. Other architecture studios involved in the complex produced a nursery, offices, a gymnasium, and commercial and communal spaces to complete a dense neighborhood, while Herzog and De Meuron contributed a residential tower for the affluent. Dwellers from all social classes would share homes and facilities on this single city block. One of Bilbao's towers was built containing units for market-rate purchase while the other two comprised subsidized units. She chose to design distinct and differentiated dwellings that occupied two levels for the subsidized units in one tower while making all plan layouts the same for the larger units to house those who can afford to purchase their homes. She described this strategy as somewhat polemical, an effort to balance the haves and have nots, all of whom would share the same communal facilities and public transportation. She noted that the experience of collaborating with this international team of architects under Herzog and De Meuron's leadership was productive and positive. Her insightful vision for clarity, simplicity, and equity driving her professional convictions for integral methods of design collaboration was reinforced by this experience. [See project documentation beginning on page 102.]

"My architecture is always emersed in its surroundings."[6]

In France, Bilbao gained valuable perspective as she built formidable professional bonds with her collaborators. She resumed practice in Mexico with an awareness of the potential for building more with less.[7] The standardized archetypal models of forty-three square feet, with small normative kitchens and other facilities resulted in one size that doesn't fit all. Her ambition to build for specific climates, geographies, rituals, and individuals stimulated an increase in her resolve to find novel solutions to domestic arrangements. Houses situated in the deserts of Chihuahua would necessarily require construction methods and formal types that differed from those in the tropical jungles of Chiapas. She decided to focus her studio's efforts on months of research into new kinds of problems, but in the process, she recognized a flaw in her method. Architects were talking only to other architects. They needed input from the very communities they aimed to house. They reached out to future residents with simple inquiries that included graphic responses, and after almost 2,000 interviews, she found a singular consistent outcome and a notion that was in conflict with their assumptions: that people wanted a house that looked like a house and that had an archetypal shape and appeared to be complete even if desires for expansion remained. Typical hand-built homes in the region had flat roofs with rebars exposed toward the sky in the hopes of one day adding a second floor. It was once a sign of optimism, but the vertical expansion almost never got built. Instead, this would come to signify an unfulfilled promise and failure to manifest. As a result, current homeowners began seeking a finished product that "looked like a house."

What Bilbao's team learned from these interactions has fed her work to date. Recognizing that people's needs stood at odds with the tiny houses that the state had been providing as low-income housing was an existential problem. At forty-three square feet,

Tatiana Bilbao at The Ohio State University

most families would need to add additional space, while the primary dwelling would be better received if it looked finished while also being able to evolve and satisfy aesthetic desires as it expanded. The adaptable house should also be able to accommodate a range of needs and thus called for flexibility in the organization of the floor plan and its enclosure.

Modularity would offer myriad solutions. A strategy of assembled formal parts made of local materials became the research focus of Bilbao's work. Resulting homes built in locations with differing cultures and climates from Ordos, Inner Mongolia, all the way to Chiapas, exhibited experimental models in which outdoor kitchens and dry toilets are common. She began to explore materials that afforded sustainable options local to their regions from compacted-earth bricks to wooden pallets. She exhibited her proposals at the 2015 Chicago Architectural Biennial and was soon commissioned by INFONAVIT to replace twenty-three homes for those near the Mexican border town at Acuña that had been completely destroyed by a tornado which had also damaged an additional 580 houses. Solidity was essential for the replaced houses in that vulnerable location, so the new homes were constructed with concrete and cement block. Bilbao has recognized that the ways in which residents are now painting and adapting their new homes is a sign of ownership and relative design success. [See project documentation beginning on page 60.]

Teaching (with) Tatiana

These experimental buildings and planning endeavors that resulted from Bilbao's research into how people really live provided fertile territory for the subjects of our students' scholarship. Graduate students are ready to take on problems critical to their generation, and they seek professional guidance. The modular dwelling exercise is not new, but Bilbao's research invited rethinking the essence of the home to accommodate spaces of production that include food preparation, shared informal care, and often small industries for economic security. Gracious rooms, functions, and appliances need not follow a singular formula. If each resident has the flexibility to organize her dwelling spaces, she can personalize her place of habitation to suit her unique family needs and aesthetic sensibilities, and eventually, perhaps, have more control over the care economy and her role in it.

As we prepared to co-teach the seminar about her practice, Tatiana and I met by phone to discuss the range of topics, readings, and pedagogy with strategies that would best suit our joint objectives. We agreed on a format. Students would form groups of three to four students each to research her buildings, urban proposals, exhibits, and projects. We framed a series of eight topics, each providing a lens through which to read selected texts from architectural and environmental theory, scrutinize her notions and artifacts, then present the findings to Tatiana during her campus visit for critical dialogue.

As we sought common ground, I proposed topics gleaned from Bilbao's built projects and recent presentations in web-posted lectures. Tatiana was engaged, responsive, and encouraging, and our discussion flowed easily. These topics would provide the structure for our syllabus with expectations articulated in its framework to support a series of sessions that would build toward our time together when Tatiana would join the seminar in person. Student research would begin with a series of readings by authors that included Elise Iturbe, Dolores Hayden, Pier Vittorio Aureli, Martino Tattara, Maria Shéhérazade Giudici, Sylvia Federici, Stefan Gruber, Hannah Arendt, Naomi Klein, and others. Topics were initially conceived as follows:

1. *Collage as a mode of representation* would open discussion about digital hyper-fluency in communicating prospective spaces and its detractors. Client communications, Bilbao had learned, remained open with more creative input if drawings were collaged with process-driven hand-made fluency rather than rendered toward a presumed reality.

2. *Cooperation and generosity with a focus on listening* would raise our awareness of community relationships throughout TBE's design process. Open to critique, understanding the implications of this thesis would invite an intimate look at the challenges of public works.

3. *Housing, Dwelling, and Cultural Needs* framed her built and experimental proposals within social contexts that ranged from Mexico to Mongolia and revealed the methods that tied her office output to her teaching regardless of the economic realities of the design.

4. *Land, Cities, and Planning* emphasized the scale of TBE's speculations for regional interventions, with an evolving method for assessing input from communities to be served over a long duration of environmental change.

5. *Capitalism, Cultural Capital, and the Environment* would invite political questioning of market-driven design and the causes and deterrents of "carbon form." The political and economic systems in which we build seem inflexible until we ask the right questions, as Bilbao has demonstrated.

6. *Society* requires deep consideration of the causes, effects, and implications of what we build, who actually benefits, and who profits. The role of Bilbao's architecture in the discourse, and the human values she discusses established a frame of reference to be challenged and discussed.

7. *Care and Reproductive Labor* brought forward the essence of Bilbao's current considerations even while showing ways in which our lack of architectural accommodation is rooted in our modern history of design.

8. *Collaboration*. Distinct among architectural practitioners, honest and successful co-working strategies are not created equally. Yet for Bilbao, collaboration is key to making architecture and design innovation relevant and to address our greatest urban and social problems. Bilbao's vast experience working with designers across cultures invited comparisons.

During our preliminary conversation as we discussed the list of prospective topics, Bilbao asked how far our campus was from St. Louis, Missouri. Her current housing project under construction, Olive West, involved demonstrable aspects applicable to each topic. She suggested we visit the site together. We scheduled the trip to occur during her visit to Columbus to follow our seminar presentations and discussions. As we reconsidered each proposed topic of study, Tatiana underscored the role of *collaboration*. She interjected emphatically, "I have worked with architects all over the world. U.S. architects are the most difficult to collaborate with!" When I asked why she believed this to be true she answered only "capitalism and competition," which I understood as values central to design culture in the United States that can negatively impact joint efforts. It was clear that the most important learning in this interaction for all of us would come when we were

(Not) Another Tower models at Chicago Biennial 2017

face-to-face and would have a common base of subjects and principles with a shared vocabulary. We would deepen our cultural and professional awareness as we got to know one another better.

Women's Work

There were significant overlaps between the assigned research topics, as was to be expected. Each example of Tatiana Bilbao ESTUDIO's completed buildings offered speculation from several of our frameworks simultaneously and enriched the discussions between teams. The presence of women in the home emerged as a common theme. Our method of inquiry was driven by formal and cultural critique from viewpoints informed by emergent evidence from practice and design theory. For example, capitalism, care, and reproductive labor; housing; and collage as representation dovetailed to deepen our understanding of Bilbao's critiques of domesticity and solutions for alternative models that appeared in her recent projects. Each team examined her contribution to the 2015 Chicago Biennial, which featured an innovative modular proposal aiming to provide affordable *existenz minimum* dwellings to best accommodate the evolving families of dwellers. The installation consisted of blue painted concrete and a natural wood pallet enclosure with two bedrooms, a bath, a kitchen and five-meter-tall communal space. The ensemble was priced in Mexico at $8,000. Most importantly, it could be expanded to meet the needs of a family's necessities. The places that women occupy in these and other domestic spaces would emerge as a dominant theme in our discussions.

Two years later in 2017, Bilbao was again invited to the Chicago Biennial. The focus of this Biennial was the scale of the metropolis inviting formal responses to urban density in the form of its lakefront of towers. Bilbao's submission responded directly to Chicago's formalist legacy as she departed from the familiar typology and challenged the status quo. Participants had been asked to conceive of alternatives to the "Vertical City," which resulted in seventeen physical models assembled in the Sidney R. Yates Gallery of the Chicago Cultural Center. Each proposed massing

MECCA x NGV Women in Design Commission: Tatiana Bilbao

towered over the exhibit's visitors. Descriptions by designers emphasized the expressions of their massive models with a focus on structural innovation and abstract physical characteristics. Bilbao's entry offered a critique of the canonical modernist response to dense housing and formalist tropes presented by the other entries, most of which featured variations on high-rise profiles and gridded skins but lacked specific contents. The tower models appeared structurally stable and compositionally similar while speaking the redux language of Miesian certainty. The ubiquitous tower type evoked an image of capitalist speculation striving merely for greater heights.

Tatiana's collaged skyscraper, titled *(Not) Another Tower*, tacitly but boldly challenged the isolation of elevator driven social encounters concealed within anonymous architecture. Her assemblage teetered and gained girth with its height. It felt wobbly and alive and served comparatively as a provocation. Her sixteen-foot-tall model was presented in section in contrast to most other submissions, which appeared as mere skin or structural diagram. Bilbao's vital interiors revealed possibilities for the everyday lives of social beings that seemed to spill out and draw you in. Evidence of a commitment to collaboration, her design took the form of an open framework as a "literal scaffold of ideas" to which she invited architects, artists, and students to fill the implied dwellings.[8] With shades of Koolhaas' *Delirious New York*, Bilbao brought a decidedly different grasp of the imagination for contemporary vertical urban dwelling to Chicago. In Edward Keegan's report on the exhibit for *Architect*, the image of Bilbao's tower photographed by Bruce Damonte appropriately showed a woman holding a child, both gazing up at Bilbao's grand figure.[9] The child is gesturing toward the sky.

During our semester of study rooted in the City of Care, Tatiana opened in Melbourne a massive installation reflecting on women's craft, care work, and communal spaces that are shared across cultures. The inaugural *MECCA x NGV Women in Design Commission* show, which opened October 2023, introduced her concept "*La ropa sucia se lava en casa*" (literally "Dirty clothes are washed at home"). As part of the installation, Tatiana had engaged individuals in Berlin, Melbourne, and Mexico City to prepare textiles by hand. The resulting tapestries filled the space of the gallery surrounding a replica of a public laundering basin. In a video for the show, Bilbao described the social sessions that gathered people at each locale to fabricate quilts sewn of donated materials in gatherings modeled after quilting bees. Participants discussed making and laundering the clothing that protected themselves and other activites for those for whom they cared.[10] The walls of the gallery featured loose hand drawings crafted on site and depicting the women engaged in washing, talking, and working at historic public plazas. Wall graphics showed women at work in such imagined places interwoven with Bilbao's dynamic collages. The installation in total set the historic scene of collective public women's work. The exhibition called attention to the fact that these activities were eventually privatized, individualized, and in their work made invisible, resulting in oppression of the very care work on which we all depend.

In an essay about the installation Simone LeAmon and Gemma Savio situate Bilbao's contribution in the broader domain of the architecture profession:

"Suggesting that architecture has imposed limitations on contemporary social structures, *MECCA x NGV Women in Design Commission | Tatiana Bilbao* is embedded with criticism of standardisation in architecture and construction. A challenge to the modernist trope of universal design, that is anything but inclusive, the work invites audiences to question the strict functional plans that predict how people live, mandate behavior, and exacerbate an assumed outline of how domestic spaces are occupied and by what familial model."[11]

Bilbao's response to the prompt aims to politicize and personalize the work of women and their undervalued labor. Her exhibition has wide-spread implications and sought to reach women across class and cultures. She replicated the *Lavadero of Huichapan*, an historic public laundry facility in Mexico, in the center of the large gallery. The figural mass served as the centerpiece of the show surrounded by her hand-crafted graphics and colored fabrics that invite touch in a bold act to aestheticize and elevate the people, their work, their cultural practices. Visitors to the exhibit understand that these public spaces and activities get overlooked at an immeasurable cost.

Yale Studio

Bilbao taught another of her design studios during Spring 2023 to architecture students at the Yale School of Architecture. The studio interpreted the theme of the Melbourne exhibition as inspiration for proposed interventions in the modern center of Mexico City. It becomes irresistible to interpret "*La ropa sucia se lava en casa*" (Dirty clothes are washed at home) through the similar Anglo-Saxon metaphor, "Don't air your dirty laundry in public." Privatizing is a power ploy. What we can hide we will ignore, deny, and undervalue. For the students at Yale, care labor and the role of women were made public and intentionally integrated into the civic realm as they sought to unpack the baggage of care labor. Highly experiential themes chosen by student designers drew attention to the body, cleaning, laundry, textile production, food preparation and sale, affordable housing, and childcare. As part of the studio, Yale students had traveled with Bilbao and other faculty members to Mexico City's Avenue de la Reforma, a monumental modern street that accommodates street vendors, food carts, and do-it-yourself markets. The overlap of activities exposes the boisterous vitality of everyday life that characterizes the city. The colors, smells, and vibrancy captured the students' imaginations and found its way into their proposed interventions lending depth of inquiry to their proposed projects and final presentations.

Bilbao's hand-crafted collage language of representation was evident in the students' visual performances, albeit souped up to envelop reviewers in the form of a digital extravaganza in the round. Layered images rotated around the walls of the room forcing spectators to swivel and bend to follow graphics in motion. Yet no amount of electronic magic or digital mirage could overshadow the core strength of the best conceived ideas nor elevate the weaker ones. Overall, each collaboration with Tatiana was inventive, compelling, and challenging to prescribed cultural norms, privatized ownership, and the ubiquity of undervalued hidden labor.

Tatiana's Teaching

Bilbao's work teaches. With intelligence, fortitude, clarity, and beauty she models in the classroom the open discourse and co-laboring strategy that she practices. Her principles for a simple, humane, conscious design recognize the body as the place to start. At this juncture her awareness of practices that impact the whole human condition transcends gender. From lessons about islands and archipelagos (Aureli & Shéhérazade Giudici)[12] to the detriment of carbon form (Iturbe)[13], the interrogation of *commoning* provides a vision of intentional settlements that is universally applicable to address the needs of the whole interdependent human condition.

Kloster Maria Friedenshort concept collage

Tatiana found and professes such a model in the form of the historic monastery. Her studies of simplified dwellings provide an essential way of understanding shelter that begins with the body itself. Her commission to build a new monastery for 900-year old German order led her to think about the monk's robe as the first step in designing a place for the body. The solitude, tranquility, and simplicity of the cell and the shared spaces of the cloister provide a sensual realm of the common. In lectures on the topic, Bilbao cuts from the call to worship witnessed in an empty, solemn monastic corridor to the common Mexican kitchen with many hands working and children in tow. Not all designers or viewers might immediately identify the crossover as spatially related. However, the juxtaposition and contrast can be understood to illustrate a range of dwelling alternatives resting importance on consultations with dwellers and knowing the relevant practices and rituals of everyday life as the beginning of the design process.

Meet Me in St. Louis

When Tatiana suggested that the Baumer Seminar class should visit her Olive West project, the neighborhood currently under construction along with her, I accepted without hesitation. She presented the experimental housing collaboration as a built and accessible model of her latest ideas. If she realized that she would be accommodating thirty-two visitors on her construction site, she was undaunted. We set about to include the site visit in our curriculum and assigned the students to research the project.

Emily Rau Pulitzer, founder of the nearby Pulitzer Foundation designed by Tadao Ando, had been seeking an architect for the neighborhood on West Olive Street in urban St. Louis for some time. Within the rehabilitated Central Grand Arts district, the Pulitzer Foundation sits adjacent to the Contemporary Arts Center by Allied Works. Together they flank a handsome Richard Serra sculpture. The 2008 financial crisis had seen the demise of the single-row townhouse typology in the historic neighborhood. Pulitzer's architect would be asked to conceive of a housing type that would serve contemporary dwellers who seek an urban lifestyle and wish to belong to a community at the confluence of cultural, academic, commercial, and residential activities. The abandoned area on Olive Street was ready for revitalization that would bring greater density to the area, infill vacant lots, and revive a lost community. Pulitzer sought to innovate in the area with a redistribution of public and private spaces.

Bilbao's housing research caught Emily Pulitzer's eye, and the two women formed a professional bond. Bilbao developed a general plan for the 3.3-acre, block-long stretch on Olive Street between and Vandeventer and Spring Avenues that challenged both the usual formal alignment of civic services including water and gas lines, while questioning formulas for public frontages and private backyards as fenced enclaves. Her plan for seventeen single family dwellings and a thirty-five-unit apartment building would interrupt common American expectations for private property in favor of communal grounds. Developer Stephen Trampe was still struggling with the notion when we met with him even as the model dwellings had already achieved commercial success. The Tatiana Bilbao ESTUDIO website states:

"Named after the street that it revolves around, Olive West recognizes the need for quality housing that predisposes communal development through shared spaces and aims for more inclusive ways of living. The general plan reacts to the cultural character of its inhabitants by creating its own center of production and meeting place within the historic Wolfner Library, as well as spaces of communal leisure and play positioned between the housing units."[14] Each two-story rectangular brick volume contains a single-family residence. Homes are arranged on the gridded terrain in a park-like setting without frontality, boulevards, or lawns. Instead, internal cross-navigating sidewalks link raised entryways and are framed by native low-maintenance plantings that soften the grounds. A community pool sits behind the historic library facilities.

Just as the two women aiming to affect difference found each other, Tatiana in turn found other designers that shared her formal intentions and cooperative vision. Tatiana Bilbao ESTUDIO would design the first prototypical house that would be repeated throughout the urban landscape. She invited other studios to contribute similar brick two-story houses to integrate and vary the elements in the complex. Her collaborators include MOS Architects (USA), Productora (Mexico-USA), and Estudio Macías Peredo (Mexico), among others. The preliminary home by Bilbao is described on the website:

"The design of Olive South West, a garden house inspired by the traditional dog-trot house, includes a central breezeway to ventilate the adjacent rooms during the hot and humid summers. The massing of the house is perpendicularly stacked to provide shade to the ground-floor porches while creating two roof gardens above, doubling the amount of potential outdoor living space for the family and creating various possibilities for private and public activities."[15]

The November day that we visited Olive West was sunny and 79 degrees Fahrenheit (don't get Tatiana going on the lack of use of the metric system in U.S. design!) enhancing the validity of the model and providing students with direct experiential learning through evidence. Bilbao, Pulitzer, Trampe, and Tatiana's daughter and mother each offered their own perspectives, and each verified the success of the model from four distinct points of view. Our students saw a novel settlement pattern, superb building craft, and innovative modes of design leadership, investment, and coordination. Held up as a viable model of the City of Care, Olive West and its potential iterations demonstrate that aesthetics inspire, social environments evolve, and collaboration works.

1 https://tatianabilbao.com/about
2 Tatiana Bilbao, *A House Is Not Just a House: Projects on Housing*. 32.
3 Ibid.
4 Ibid, 34.
5 "So while financial models and resale prices might be the indicator of value right now, we can imagine a better system in which value is actually determined by the quality of life in these homes." *A House Is Not Just a House: Projects on Housing*, 43.
6 Tatiana Bilbao, *A House Is Not Just a House: Projects on Housing*. 40.
7 In conversation with Jacques Herzog, Tatiana says, "You told me how important it was to use the global world we were born into to create a network, something your generation did not do. ...It has this element of the importance of the space, rather than the importance of the person behind it, so operating in a network has allowed me to create things that would not be easy to think up as one person, but also could not be built as a single person," in *Tatiana Bilbao Estudio*, 117-118.
8 Hillary Sample, *Tatiana Bilbao Estudio*, 75.
9 https://www.architectmagazine.com/design/a-more-focused-chicago-architecture-biennial_o
10 https://www.yellowtrace.com.au/tatiana-bilbao-mecca-ngv-women-in-design-commission/#gallery-15
11 https://www.ngv.vic.gov.au/essay/mecca-x-ngv-women-in-design-commission-tatiana-bilbao/
12 Pier Vittorio Aureli and Maria Shéhérazade Giudici, "Islands: The Settlement from Property to Care." *Log* 47, 175-199, Fall 2019.
13 Elise Iturbe, "Architecture and the Death of Carbon Modernity." *Log* 47, 11-23, Fall 2019.
14 https://tatianabilbao.com/projects/olive-west-masterplan
15 https://tatianabilbao.com/projects/olive-west-masterplan

Above: Olive West South; Next page: Ways of Life collage

A CONVERSATION WITH TATIANA BILBAO

The following conversation between Tatiana Bilbao, Kay Bea Jones, and students of the Knowlton School was recorded in the autumn of 2022. It has been edited for clarity.

ARCHITECTURE AND SOCIETY

KAY BEA JONES: I'd like to thank Tatiana for joining us today. We have a number of topics to cover that we think are instrumental in your work and how they relate to the current state of architecture. The students will introduce these topics by framing them against examples from your body of work and other examples. We're excited to hear how you understand your own practice in relation to these issues and how you think of your work within the larger discipline.

TATIANA BILBAO: Thank you for having me. This is a really great opportunity to reflect on the work in a way that is different from making the work. In the studio, we are always thinking deeply about what we are doing, but it's not always the case that you have an opportunity to step back and try to see things from a more distanced perspective. So, thank you, I'm looking forward to it as much as you are.

STUDENT: Good morning. We've been considering your work within the context of the role of the architect in society in general. It's a fairly broad way to begin, but I would begin by saying that architecture shapes our prospects and dispositions while reinforcing and naturalizing them. The built environment that we make and modify reflects and guides our imperatives as a society and as individuals. There's a distinction between architecture that reflects current imperatives and those that challenge and engage them. Political philosophies and design philosophies have evolved many times over the course of history, and we might say that the numerous crises we face now indicate that the built environment is going to change again, possibly in a rather radical way. So maybe a first question is, "Where do we go from here?"

In a very primitive way, architecture can be defined as the basic making of shelter. While true, this definition is also clearly insufficient in almost any context. Architecture is many more things: property for profit, spaces of efficiency, objects of wonder, political ambition, places for the public good. Sometimes architecture considers the lives of those who will use it and sometimes it does not.

You said at one point that, "Architects tend to think that we know how people should live and act in any place. Architecture, on the contrary, should become a little more understanding." We thought that was a pretty powerful quote in regard to issues such as these.

The Line in Saudi Arabia is probably the most recent example of this. This is a megastructure that is more or less completely ignorant of the site context around it—perhaps deliberately so. There are many questions around this project that beget more questions. Are architects okay working with this government entity? If so, should we be critical of that? Will there be agency over personal space or will the government mandate conditions for occupation?

With respect to your work, Minimum Housing for Ocoyoacac in Apan, Mexico, is one of thirty-two rural housing prototypes constructed for the Informative Investigation Center for Sustainable Development and is designed with economic and material efficiency in mind by using as few components as possible while being as adaptable as possible. The modular design and minimum of components keeps the cost low and allows for the configuration to be based on the needs of the residents.

Lyon La Confluence presents a typology that serves various populations and addresses needs from individuals with differing backgrounds and lifestyles. We will talk more about this later, but the enabling of social interaction through the facade and layout are among the goals of this housing project.

Silica II attempts to break a barrier that has been constructed within the expanse of a typical city by injecting a newfound—and maybe lost—sense of community by focusing on one site and organizing unfamiliar scales of space to enable new relationships between those spaces. These spaces become combinations of the public and the private, about which you have said, "We designed a building that is not divided by corridors, but instead is thought of

Apan Housing: Ocoyoacac Minimum Housing

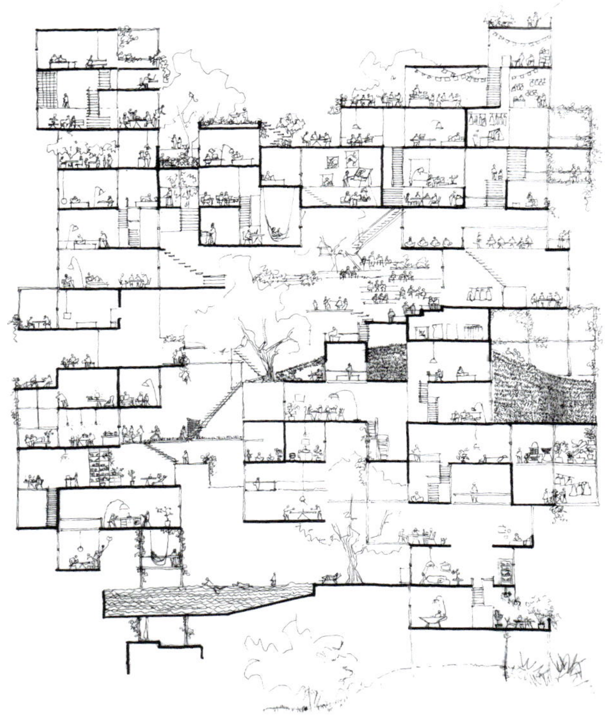

Silica II section illustration

Lyon La Confluence model

Acuña Housing prototype

Ways of Life illustration

(Not) Another Tower collage

Olive West illustrated site plan

Tatiana Bilbao ESTUDIO home page illustration

as spaces that foster a possibility of different types of relationships between neighbors."

Housing+ focuses on things such as modularity, adaptability, and providing inhabitants a way to express their own ideas about domesticity. The project enables varied social and cultural ideals while providing a dignified way of life. This is something that is not always afforded to people based on broader societal norms and the divisions that exist with those norms, whether bureaucratic or political or otherwise. This project seems like a step toward framing architecture as a human right as opposed to simply thinking of it as housing for the masses, capital, or property. It is a project that pays attention to and enables domestic labor, which is another topic that we're going to address in more detail later.

Ways of Life deals with the idea of creating a space that is not determined by function. Typically, housing is half living space and half (reproductive) working space. Spaces are determined and functionally-fixed based on assumptions that we all use and signify spaces in the same way. This means that we come in having predetermined what and where kitchens and bathrooms—for example—are or should be placed. In this project, every space could be a kitchen, or every space could be a bathroom, or it could be that the house inhabitants decide to have no kitchen, or a bathroom that is atomized within the house. Here we are looking at the house as more than just a place of rest and as more than just a collection of utilitarian spaces; we are looking at the house as a collection of spaces that allow activities, emotions, experiences, and memories to happen as the inhabitant lives it.

Olive West is meant to provide private housing in St. Louis. The project is part of a search for a more communally-oriented and local way of living in the Midwest and as an alternative to current urban models or dated suburban models of domesticity. It aspires to be the starting point for a new urban fabric here and hopes to set an example for other developments nearby or elsewhere.

(Not) Another Tower applies your design philosophy to a tower in order to create a matrix of new possibilities within a relatively established typology. It's a powerful argument and very inspiring. If one is not thinking about new ways to build and new ways to create communities, then one is not going to make them a reality. There's a huge contrast between your proposal and existing towers and is a very successful critique of the vertical building.

One project that we're all very interested in and very speculative about is the Neuzelle Monastery. You have previously presented images and audio clips of life in a monastery and how much it revised your understanding of domestic space, specifically the importance of scale, size, and ritual. This is perhaps the biggest challenge to the binary understanding of architecture and space, public versus private, or served versus service.

In short, it's among the roles of architects to care about how people could create their own lives, and, by extension, to care about how we live as a society in common ways. In a broad sense, architects must advocate for the end users of the world by designing in a thoughtful and intentional way that challenges and engages our current society's goals through collaboration with communities and colleagues. We need to identify values that guide the transformation of our society into a system that reflects our needs and desires. Only in this way will our built environment be able to enforce the imperatives of people, families, and communities.

That is a lot of set up. Maybe a direct question to get started? Your website homepage is a city map. It's a collection of projects and places within the structure of a larger collective environment. Is this a philosophical or design statement? How do you approach ideas of being part of a particular place or larger community while operating in cultures that cherish building wealth, maintaining ownership, having more assets, and arguably, sharing less?

BILBAO: Thank you so much. The website is both a philosophical statement and a design statement. I believe that architecture is what shapes the way we live in cities, and every single piece we design adds an element to that collective collage that every city is. Even if we only add a single bench, we are shaping the city in which we are building. On the other hand, the website is a drawing of the city because we think of the city as the sum of its architectures; we see it working as a group and as a collection of things but that are intrinsically connected—or disconnected—from each other. For me, it is very important to see every piece we add into any context as one that enables, collaborates, triggers, or adds possibility to a larger context.

In a way, I also like to think that it is not only these connections or relationships that every building produces, but how each of them serve both the collective and the single body that will inhabit them. Maybe that part is not reflected in the image of the city on our web page, but our intention with the hand drawing and the diversity you see on that image is to reveal that one of the studio's premises is that each building should be a platform to accept any manner of inhabiting it since we are all so different. Everything and everyone has a particular personality.

One of our big challenges is exactly embedded in that last line of thought. We have always asked ourselves how it is that architecture can become the platform for anyone to inhabit this planet. How can we get as many as possible to be involved in the creation of their own place and their own space?

This is part of why I challenge the notion of the skyscraper with *(Not) Another Tower* for the Chicago Biennial. Structurally and programmatically, they hold hundreds or thousands of people, and none of them are represented because skyscrapers are fairly monolithic buildings that are often defined by a single move or gesture. They're not made by a single person—because a lot of people are involved in producing architecture—but they are still often a single gesture that holds many things and, in the end, nothing but the building itself is represented there. I still like to think that the construction and development of the idea could be done more collectively. Our proposal was based on the idea that a tower could allow for more people to be represented. I've always felt that there is a necessity for places or buildings to be more about a process that builds itself in different moments in time, in different aesthetic definitions, in different ways, for different people. Places emerge in different ways. In many developed countries, a city is planned out and infrastructure comes first. In countries like Mexico, people come first. The built environment exists and then infrastructure is incorporated. Building vertically requires a little more planning. In these cases, perhaps infrastructure arrives first and then it becomes built over years and years. We have had many discussions about how we could extend our cities in a vertical way. Obviously, we now understand that extending them in a linear or horizontal way creates certain problems.

With Ways of Life, it was important to understand the notion of self-representation in a space. It was meant to be an architecture that could become a platform for anybody to create their own way of living. The brief asked for a space that would respond to or facilitate new ways of life. For me, these new ways of life were assumed (by the brief) to be referring to those who provide productive labor and domesticity in one place. The brief assumed that this was a new condition.

With the pandemic, working and living in the same space became much more present. But to assume that the two conditions are separate aspects of life that occur in different locations is wrong because home is and always has been a place of work (reproductive work, which is necessary for each of us to exist). But the house is also where much of the population on earth still does its productive job, especially in rural areas. Since the industrial revolution, we have intended to separate these two realms, but that's only happened in the urban centers and now, with the shift in work types, that distinction is also getting blurred. For me, the house is simply not a place for mere rest in almost any capacity. Work has been done in our houses and in our homes since the start of humanity.

The statement of Ways of Life also pointed to something that we tend to assume in the Western world, which is that everyone lives or should aspire to live as we do. For me, it's about recognizing that there are many ways of life. Some of them will obviously include working productively and reproductively in the same place. Some of them just involve reproductive work while others only need to incorporate productive work. With farms, productive and reproductive labor are kind of mixed.

So, there are many different ways of life. Each of us plans and lives in a different way even though we have very similar built structures in which this happens. This strikes me as odd. I'm less interested in focusing on how to create a platform for domestic labor and more interested in creating a platform so that anyone can design for their mode of living. That was the purpose of Ways of Life.

STUDENT: Wasn't there a mandate for building a physical house?

BILBAO: As mentioned before, the brief asked for a house that could respond to new ways of life, and it described these new ways of life by saying that, "We're going to be working from home more." The truth is that we've been working from home forever both productively and reproductively. The brief asked for a very specific house that would hold a living space, a kitchen, a bathroom, and a space to work. It described six different types of spaces. I think one of the problems is that, as architects, we tend to design spaces that are defined for specific uses, and they are becoming more and more detailed and specialized. But they are also becoming more narrowly understood. Such spaces are hard to transform for different types of use. A bathroom is the most extreme case. A bathroom, when you design it and if you live like that, needs to be used in a very specific way.

The powerful Western model of society thinks that it has found the comfortable way of living for every human on this planet. But I believe we have forgotten that not one single human being on this planet is the same or inhabits the same space as others. We inhabit specific geographical conditions with very specific social, cultural, economic, or political relationships and connections to the environment. For example, with Housing+ we understood that in Mexico there is no sewage system in certain rural areas. How can you design a house with a bathroom that needs sewage and that functions in the same manner as those in urban large areas that have that infrastructure? It makes no sense. Dry bathrooms are constructed outside of the house for obvious reasons in these cases. Thinking that the whole world has the same capacities and same infrastructure—or that it ought to be enlightened to do so—is ignorant. On the other hand, I would say that a much more sustainable system in rural Mexico makes sense, as opposed to thinking that we need to bring them infrastructure because they're poor and have no sewage infrastructure. No. In these cases, it's much better to implement sewage biodigesters that are much friendlier to the environment. They don't need a process of opening the earth and installing infrastructure, because then you have to place tubes in the earth that take that sewage where? With a single move of putting a traditional Western bathroom in, you are defining the type of environment you are creating in significant ways.

STUDENT: You either connect it to the larger network or you must make a whole new hub system.

BILBAO: Exactly. But if this is a rural area where houses are scattered all over and they have their own system of biodigesters, it's much better. If we create houses that only have bathrooms that take sewage, then the sewage needs to come out. And then we're talking about plugging into systems that have a hard time accommodating change or variation and that require a lot of resources of every type to be built and sustained. Perhaps this is one of the problems we are encountering with climate change? We assume that we can force or develop new models according to old systems. I just don't think that some of the issues—whether they're as small as plumbing in rural communities or as large as climate change—are going to be like that. I think some of these issues are going to require real systemic changes of thought, expectation, and consideration of lifestyle. It will mean changes in economic, political, and social models and practices. Unlearning and relearning in the face of new stresses or contexts is hard. So far, we're not doing a very good job.

KAY BEA JONES: As an example, modern expectations of what hygiene means is one size fits all without recognition of what alternatives have been going on for centuries.

BILBAO: Yes. Another problem that we tried to address with Housing+ is that the housing needed to comply with the code. The code in Mexico is very specific in that a house will not be called or treated as a house without meeting certain conditions. It says that a house must be, at minimum, a space that has a kitchen, a bathroom, two bedrooms, and a living room. And that's it. If a house doesn't comply with those divisions, it cannot be called a house. In every country of the world there are similar rules.

In this case, these people cook communally. Why would they need a kitchen inside? Second, the food in Mexico is super rich. It's charged with culture and it's charged with history. It's charged with rooting yourself to your own surroundings. It depends on where you grow up there. Food is rich in spices and rich in flavor and sometimes cannot be cooked on a kitchen counter inside a living space. The smell of the food permeates sleeping spaces, sometimes for days or weeks. So really, we need to understand that imposing an idea of how to live onto the rest of the world is very colonial.

There's also an assumption about rooms. Some live and sleep in rooms and in flat beds and that's fine. But assuming that everyone does, or that everyone needs to do the same is discriminating. A simple and easy example is that a part of the Maya community in Mexico had adopted the hammock as a place to sleep 500 years ago. It was a simple and practical response to their way of living and to the geographical and environmental conditions of the place they inhabit. And why do they sleep in hammocks? People often think it's because they're poor, but it's the opposite. It's because they are very clever and in tune with their environment. The average temperature in the area where the Mayans live is very hot and humid year-round. A hammock allows for airflow around a body and the maintenance of a particular comfort threshold as defined by their culture and habits. Not only that, but because of the humidity and the temperature, there are some serious bug issues. When you have a bed, those bugs can get inside, and when you have a hammock they don't. And guess what? When you create a space that requires a bed, you impose onto the occupant a piece of furniture that is completely foreign to them. Then you have a whole new set of problems. Now you need mechanical or artificial air regulation because obviously it's going to be difficult for them to sleep like that in this temperature. You're potentially creating a health problem that, as it turns out, will require a robust health system that comes from the larger institutional government. So, the hammock becomes a bed that requires a room that necessitates air conditioning and can lead to a dependency on a state health system. None of these foreign things would be necessary if we simply understood the context that the Mayans were operating in and why. Instead, we tend to make assumptions or impose forms of development or "improvement."

There's an act of colonization that is inherent at numerous steps in the making of architecture. Building anything anywhere is already an act of colonization in basic form: it is taking land and imposing something on top of it. But if we also push specific forms and specific ways of using these forms, it begins to cross over into colonizing those who use it. We have to begin making efforts to understand how to increase responsibility for and respect of the land and the people who occupy it. I've realized that we need to do a better job of listening and paying attention.

STUDENT: Something you said early on is that primarily what we're doing is providing for people. It made me think of—

BILBAO: Let me interrupt, though. The term *provide* is difficult for me and it's maybe not the word that I wanted to use. For me it's hard to unlearn the language that we sometimes use by habit, but I'm skeptical of the notion that architects actually *provide*. I would correct that to say that we should consider how we can immerse ourselves in a system of allowing anyone to create or re-create their own lifestyle or ambitions. The idea of us *providing* something implies that we have a special power over something. I trip over my own words and thoughts every day because I was born into this system, I was educated in it, and I have worked in it. But I'm trying to learn and unlearn every day. I try to teach myself and correct myself every day.

STUDENT: I was thinking of *providing* in terms of being able to offer a service. We refer to doctors as providers and they typically serve individuals and hopefully help them with their lives. I was thinking of *providing* more in that sense and not in the sense that architects have some inherent final say or objective wisdom.

BILBAO: How can we offer the things that we know (as architects) and the things that we've learned to someone who can use them to add to their own knowledge in such a way that would improve their capacity for action? Or how can we build something that comes from our own understanding and allows for the growth of the understanding of those that use what is made? I think that's the right question.

STUDENT: When you're designing for other cultures that you're not as knowledgeable about, how do you inform yourself about it? Do you start by talking with those who the project is going to serve?

BILBAO: It's a good question. In the beginning, I thought that truly understanding was a goal, but then I realized that we never truly understand. We never actually understand how anybody else is going to live. I started understanding that it's not about me being immersed in the context, but rather it's about making architecture that can become a platform for anybody to live in. In the case of Lyon, it was difficult because it's in France. In France, the building code is unbelievably determined. For example, the position that a bed needs to exist in a room is determined with respect to the window and the door. I have experienced many codes in many places, but this is the most restrictive code that I've encountered. It imposes a specific way of life. I don't think it's a good thing, despite the general good intentions of building codes. Lyon is social housing, and the social housing system there is somewhat generous by many standards. Many of the units are made to rent (in a subsidized manner) to immigrants that often come from different French colonies. These individuals and families have lived in completely different ways than those they are introduced to as it is specifically imposed by the building codes. So, in reality it's not generous at all, because it doesn't consider the way one might inhabit a space, but forces them to inhabit in the same way that the French do. I think a good thing to do would be to create platforms for opening things up in terms of these policies. That should also be our task. Architects are partially responsible for creating these policies. Perhaps we could create policies that are open to more varied manners of domesticity rather than making everyone live the way someone thought everyone should live. We shouldn't tell people that they have to forget about the structures of domesticity that may exist in their culture and to simply get with the program. It's a systemic and philosophical change that needs to happen.

PRODUCTIVE AND REPRODUCTIVE LABOR

STUDENT: I think it would be good for us to define productive and reproductive labor so that we're on the same page. Reproductive labor is all the work that is required to sustain life. This includes all the work we need to stay healthy, childbearing, cooking and eating, care of the sick or disabled, washing and laundry, cleaning, planning, and how to take care of all of it. Productive labor is, in general, when you are producing money; it's generally been considered—since the industrial revolution—as the work that you do, "outside of the house." Understanding the evolution of the house and the kitchen might be helpful here.

The history of the kitchen has almost always focused on the hearth, which has represented safety, warmth, food, security, storytelling, and socializing. In the beginning, a fire in a cave or out in the open created a center for food preparation and survival. The Neolithic site of Skara Brae in Scotland includes eight homes that exhibit a very thought-out plan that is replicated in each and—in each case—the hearth is in the middle, there are two beds, and storage spaces throughout. Other cultural examples include long houses with a central fire in the middle. There are some examples of common hearths shared among many individuals or families. There are some hearths that were clearly used for communal food production.

In Greek, the word *oikos* is best translated as, "household." It refers to the space of domestic life but also to the management of that space. The term recognizes that the family is a collective that lives together and works toward a common need. Domestic spaces were divided into public spaces and secluded spaces, with certain populations (women and slaves) pushed to spaces in the back.

The Roman *domus* follows a similar standard of expressing ownership of private land or private space as a status symbol. There were shops up front and one could see through a vestibule into an atrium, where business would be done and visitors could engage with the owners. The kitchen was pushed completely into the back and was where all the domestic labor was done. The development of merchant classes in the Renaissance accelerated and embedded the separation between work and domesticity. Terraced housing

Frankfurt kitchen

in London developed in the seventeenth century maintained the separation by keeping the kitchen and the working areas in the basement and the residences above.

For the modern rationalist, the kitchen became a central living space as well as labor space. Christine Frederick was an economist in the early twentieth century and the first to focus on the idea of the functional kitchen. It was effective because the components of the kitchen were organized to be as efficient as possible. It was a systematic approach that sought to iron out any personal or cultural inefficiencies, which were seen as detriments to getting things done quickly.

Existenzminimum was the formal systematization, standardization, and homogenization of the *Deutscher Werkbund* that sought to make living as efficient as possible, whether spatially, economically, or in terms of lighting and natural ventilation. The Frankfurt kitchen is perhaps the famous model of kitchen efficiency, and one that carries through a lot of contemporary kitchen design. So, the trajectory of all of this has been a pretty clear one: a focus on efficiency and the relegation of certain roles or jobs to a minimized presence or space.

La Chalmeta (Barcelona) by Pau Vidal + Vivas Arquitectos

However, there are some examples across the world that offer alternatives. In South America—particularly in Guyana—the indigenous people use cassava as a primary food source. From the cassava, they create a drink called *kasiri*, which is a beverage that's produced by the matriarchs of the community in outdoor kitchens. Throughout the day, everyone in the community comes by, drinks this, and has conversations about the day. In Italy, there is a similar practice by grandmothers who socialize with their friends in the streets and produce pasta throughout the day for all to share, sell, and help supplement their family income. These are matriarchs in a community creating a spatial and experiential center where they're participating and organizing these reproductive tasks. Sometimes these women receive their mail in their established location on the street as opposed to at their home because they see it—this shared public space—as an extension of their home.

I think there is clearly a growing architectural and social interest in changing the understanding of what constitutes the domestic. La Chalmeta in Barcelona by Pau Vidal + Vivos Arquitectos is a repurposed building. The corridor is used to create encounters; it's outside of the courtyard. It was developed through participatory design with the people in the community who decided what types of space they wanted. The ground floor is a collective domain with shared kitchens. This project is another example of dealing with corridors and interstitial space as a way of facilitating types of change and upending some established norms or conventions. There are views into the living units and shared spaces that I think lend a sense of community. It's a way to create smaller local environments within the larger project. Minimum Housing for Ocoyoacac deals with labor in the home differently.

Apan Housing: Ocoyoacac Minimum Housing

In your projects, how have you approached this notion of the labor that is produced there? How do you address these particular topics from an economic angle when working with clients? If it's a more expensive house—as in the case of Olive West—is it different?

BILBAO: We try to approach it the same way, but we take stock of the different cultural and social aspects. It's more than just high-end or low-end, although that is part of the social difference. The Ways of Life house is high end. Other projects are in relatively or objectively poor communities. We try to think about it as the differences that we all have politically, socially, economically, culturally, and personally.

I think that trying to define the history and evolution of the Western house is a difficult one. There are entire academic careers dedicated to trying to do this. But I think we can say that part of the history of the last two centuries in the Western world has been about making the house a "more efficient machine" for the reproductive caregiver without recognizing it. Cooking and cleaning and raising children is very hard work and requires a lot of time and energy. This has been done collectively through history, but as the decades pass, society has relegated it more to sole individuals. And this is also a matter of efficiency, because the fewer people we have doing that, the more we can have in wage labor positions. Even then, it's a complete fallacy because we can't produce without being taken care of or providing care. Cooking collectively requires a lot of preparation and organization. When one person does it, the same thing is true, but it's just one person who needs to wrap their mind around it. Planning all the resources to prepare it, serve it, and clean it is a real task. And we do all have to eat.

I would say that there's no way we could talk about equality in the world if we don't talk about reproductive labor as a form of labor that is on equal footing with other types, period, regardless of who does it. Today, it's done by women 95% of the time. If we could balance that out, we could get closer to equality. The truth is that we are far from achieving this, whether statistically or in terms of cultural acceptance. It is hard to imagine it as anything other than a lot of exploitative work that is not paid. We have a long way to go on this.

Care is the necessary labor we need to perform in order to exist and to produce in the other capacities in which we work. But it's not paid for, and when it is paid for, it's typically very poorly compensated. Think about the wages we often pay food workers, cleaning people, home health or assisted living workers.

It's really as if the Western house became a tool for making that labor more efficient and allowed more people to be productive outside of the house. But then the weight of all those productive people depends on those people doing the reproductive labor at home efficiently. No one can work productively without that other work being done. None of us. We need to be nurtured, we need to be educated, we need to sleep well, we need to be healthy, and we need to have our clothes ready and clean to go to work. All that happens without being recognized and without being paid for in almost every scenario. All of that subsidizes the workforce. There are many communities that still hold care as a communal act. Not necessarily in a more equal way, but in a more communal way. We should think as society in both directions, and how we can become more equal while embracing the basic needs of the other that we have as humans. This means embracing the communal.

In some ways, what we have done has followed on the ideas of using machines to make work less visible and less recognizable. We could say that the machine of architecture or the house does this. I am conscious that architecture can't change society, but I do think it can limit its agency, and this is what I think happens specifically in the typology of the house.

During the pandemic I thought I could start promoting a different way of doing household work in my own building. I live in one of six units. I thought it was the perfect scale for a small community to share things easier. I started thinking about making a proposal to all the neighbors for sharing care.

JONES: There you are, colonizing the neighborhood.

BILBAO: It's kind of true. But I wanted to organize the tasks of homeschooling, cooking, and laundry—one day assigned per person—to have five or six days of being able to do our wage-earning jobs. When I started figuring out how and where we would do this, I realized it was not going to be possible. Where do we cook? In my kitchen? I cannot cook for 20 people every day as things are set up. Can you cook one dinner for 20 people every day in your kitchen? Then I thought we could reduce it to just taking care of the children. Where? In my living room where I work? It's set up for that? Okay, well maybe just the washing of clothes? How do I wash clothes for everyone? It ended up with me just asking everyone, "I'm going to the supermarket, does anyone need anything?" (laughter) That was our cooperation because we didn't have spaces to do any of these things collectively. I'm not saying that they should be done only collectively, but they should be able to happen collectively. This is one of the ways architecture limits our capacities.

JONES: Here we often ask questions about what happens when nobody pays for this type of shared space you're speaking of. Who owns collective space? Who is responsible for it? And yet, if you have great public space that is safe and well designed to accommodate what families are doing, these things happen

Hunter's Point Masterplan collage

organically, right? I think the idea of matriarchs in public is fascinating. Historically, Italian cities have spaces where people are comfortable. It happens because architecture and culture accommodate one another, express one another, and enable scenarios to happen. It doesn't have to be taught to people, it comes extremely naturally.

BILBAO: If two parents work full time, the shared labor model can become a problem. Who cares for people if this is the situation? Who cares for children? Who cares for elders? Who cares for themselves? Who produces your food? This is what happens, for example, in societies where that condition of not respecting reproductive care surges. For example, take New York City. What do you have there? Restaurants, childcare facilities, nursing homes, laundry services, take-out services. All of these things require money in order to have your reproductive care done. You need more money to take care of yourself, and you need to pay for everything. New York enables all sorts of cultural conditions that are amazing—even novel in a lot of ways—but there are other sides of that coin.

JONES: And now you can't afford your apartment, so you move up to the Hudson Valley and you lose proximity to your connections and your commute time just went way up. The economic-lifestyle system happens over a long time, but it has scripted us in all sorts of ways.

But there's something else. We, the Anglo-Saxon culture, suffer loneliness at a level that is uncommon across cultures. There are many stages of life. The best part for many is young adulthood or college when you live communally or close to communally. As life goes on, you may see grandparents or elders who end up alone or isolated. Perhaps they aren't able to be with people on a daily basis or have access to conversation or dialogue. There are no mutual dependencies. When you have public environments where people naturally support each other, there's satisfaction and wellbeing. It's not an economic thing. You can't put a price tag on it. Considering everything economically forces the placing of value on things. When you do that, you lose a lot.

BILBAO: Exactly. That's that point. We create architecture that serves a productive system. We don't have an architecture that serves the care system. That is exactly the question we have been asking ourselves for a while. We started with a very narrow vision, thinking that if only we could produce singular spaces that provide a shelter at an affordable price for everyone, we would be addressing the issue. But we never questioned the model of that shelter. Now we understand that the deeper problem is the typology.

CAPITALISM, CULTURAL CAPITAL, AND ENVIRONMENT

STUDENT: Capitalism is defined as an economic and political system by which a country's trade and industry are controlled by private owners for profit. Cultural capital is defined as the social assets of a person that promote social mobility, especially in stratified societies. Environmentalism is the concern about and action aimed at protecting the environment. We're at an all-time low in terms of public development in the United States, and the vast majority of building is happening in the private sector.

Offices often have to work for those who have the money and for those willing to pay for the building or production. Reiner de Graaf, responding to the economist Thomas Piketty, posits the reality that wealth is now exceeding a return on labor, with the architectural worker being more of a producer for the client rather than a problem solver or an individual designer. De Graaf posits that instead of modern and postmodern, we might actually have created a pre- and post-capital system. Buildings are going from building-to-use to building-to-own.

In the near future, returns on wealth through ownership will exceed wealth of a lifetime on paper, which is contributing to social inequity and taking away any chance of social mobility. What can architects do? Buildings no longer require intention but rather a generic desirability in economic terms.

Territorio de Gigantes model

Territorio de Gigantes rendering

We did an analysis of some of your projects, along with a few others, to look at the ways in which architects are working within a limiting economic system and simultaneously making an impact on cultural capital and environmentalism. We are going to be looking at projects at various scales, starting with the Hunter's Point Master Plan.

This large-scale remediation plan seeks to rectify historic inequities in the Bayview neighborhood in San Francisco and to restore the land to a livable standard after years of destruction by PG&E. This is a project that highlights human-centered design and prioritizes community involvement. There are mixed use spaces, various densities, and multiple housing types. The community was heavily involved in the closing and dismantling of the plant and are still involved in the design process through the Hunters Point Program. The programming fits into a wheel of life and considers how current and future residents live and can remain part of the neighborhood. Environmentally, the heavily industrial site is being restored, and through collaboration with landscape architects, benchmarks were set for sustainable practices related to energy, water, and climate resilience. Standards have been set before construction and require developers to meet them.

Territorio de Gigantes is located in Aguascalientes, Mexico. It covers a massive area on the eastern edge of the city and is in direct contrast to the western edge that is already well developed. The project is a collaboration with five other architects. There's a checkerboard arrangement of the general master plan. The checkerboard has a series of similarly shaped or similarly sized solids and voids, which is meant to promote a sense of community between the shared and neutral spaces. The layout includes low-income housing, care spaces, community markets, and open areas for recreation and sports. The goal of the project at the smaller scale is for occupants to have a sense of communal use without forcing collectivity onto them. In many cases, the users aren't used to this size of a building. Some stairs are sculptural and highlighted and shared for chance encounters.

La Confluence in Lyon is part of a larger master plan coordinated by Herzog & de Meuron in 2007. Your part of the project comprises three buildings, two of which are for social housing and one of which is for market-rate housing. Formally, the buildings of the master plan are arranged around an inward-facing public courtyard. This creates a perimeter that allows for a sense of security, but not exclusion. It's very permeable around the city block. The buildings themselves have similar interior palettes to create an identity for the community, but they celebrate the formal differences along the carved corners of the buildings. Economically, the intermingling of social dynamics promotes a community independent of economic status. Having the two types of housing next to each other normalizes social housing by making it visible, and it encourages more traditional community members used to private living to participate in a co-living community.

All of this brings us to the question of who we—as architects—are working for? How can we widen our client base and design for those beyond the financiers of projects? There's the conventional idea that architecture is about making buildings, but I would argue that it's really more about solving problems and establishing contexts. How do we ensure that the architect is valued in these ways and that we get paid? Is it necessarily a question of capitalism?

BILBAO: We're a part of the system. We need to get paid in order to take care of ourselves, our family, and our employees. One of the issues, as you pointed out, is related to land and private property. That's the basis of capitalism and the basis of the problem. If you think of the pencil towers in New York City, they are a monument to this moment in life that we are living. That plot of land is so small yet is used to extract huge amounts of money.

These are the precedents that set a standard of exploitation of land and extraction of value. The friction comes into play when we realize that architecture is a necessary tool to inhabit the planet for any human being. We need the land to allow us to build shelters that protect and inspire our lives to be lived. When you use land in such exploitative ways, that is the problem. In France, a lot of land is public, and the system allows you to develop it for a certain period of time and to make money from that built matter. But the government retains the right to develop space for the public. It could be seen as a less greedy practice, but when we get into deeper topics—such as where the wealth comes from—you will again often find exploitation and discrimination as a result. In the Lyon project, the city launched a request for a team that would develop the projects on public land. They looked for the best bid based on what the city was asking for, which was housing that would be both rented and sold. Potential developers built teams of experts in every field (including architects) to come up with a proposal.

JONES: In other words, the developer wins the competition with a team. They get to make money only on a portion of the development on the property and they never own the land. The government always owns the land and they're going to facilitate the building of social housing as part of the whole project.

BILBAO: The companies that administer the social housing are not for-profit companies. They're partially public and partially private. But they do rent and manage the properties. The government subsidizes the tenant to rent one of those units. If someone lives there for five years and pays rent correctly via subsidies, they can buy the property. But the building manager-owner can only sell 50 percent of the building. They have to keep 50 percent as rentable.

JONES: That's such an important part of this project because it helps to keep communities together. If you start to make too much money to be eligible for affordable housing, you can buy your house and stay. You've gotten to know your neighbors and your community, and this allows you to let your kids grow up there or for you to grow old there, and so on. But since only 50 percent can be privately owned, the building is always part of the network of social housing.

BILBAO: It's that, but it's also more than just maintaining communities. When you have a building next door in which the apartments cost a million euros, it does something else. The system in France is such that you have the same public services that are used by everybody. Schools and hospitals and other services are commonly shared. This means that the person who has no job and earns nothing and has rent subsidized will have their children going to school with the children of the person that is paying a lot of money to live there. They go to the same hospital and buy food in the same market. This really allows for more equitable relationships to emerge in the city. It's not perfect, but they're trying. What they're trying with projects like this is to integrate more of society. It's an admirable model.

In the United States or Mexico, if you don't grow up in a place where your food is nurturing, you can't grow healthy. If you don't go to a school that has resources, you will not learn the same as someone who does, and you will not have access to the same colleges or the same jobs. How does this even approach balancing out? Is it even interested in doing so? I think that's a question we have to ask of those who make policy. Imagine if you didn't eat well, literally, for years. Imagine if you haven't slept well or with a sense of security. These things are happening as a regular occurrence. Imagine if you didn't have the same schooling conditions as others. This goes way beyond effort or ability. This is a cultural, structural, and political inequity, and perhaps is done for the benefit of those who profit, whether explicitly or by habit.

I was going to say this before with Hunter's Point, but when you build something on top of the land, the land gains value. In Hunter's Point, one of the big challenges is that San Francisco is one of the most expensive cities in the world, and real estate is more expensive than ever. In this case, this part of the city was left out because it was deeply industrial. Now it's changing. The moment you remove a polluting industry, you invite gentrification.

If it's a super capitalist system like San Francisco, removing industry expands the population that lives there, but it's going to expel those who were living next to the place immediately beforehand. So, you relieve the burdens of living next door to a polluting neighbor, but at the cost of raising the value of the land and, thus, the rent and the cost of living there. What do we do? This exact issue is what allows the public system of France to do whatever they want to do for the public good; they don't give value to the land in the same way because the land is removed from the market system. It doesn't produce what is happening in New York City.

We need to figure out a way to think outside of that context, especially now that production modes are completely changing as well. I think it's a good moment to reconsider the city because it's been laid out as a platform for efficiency in order to produce. How can we turn around and reconsider the city laid out as a platform for care? Is it possible to create that city on top of the one we have? Or is the form so embedded with the figure that we cannot reverse it? It is a situation that needs more than architecture, but architecture can be a part of it. These are some of the questions that we try to address in the office and with our partners.

COOPERATION, LISTENING, GENEROSITY

STUDENT: I'd like to talk about issues of cooperation, listening, and generosity. The Pilgrim's Route is a religious route that marks a traditional journey performed during Holy Week, which is typically the week before Easter. This path is travelled by millions of believers to give praise and thanks. The master plan was introduced to provide better connections and services like bathrooms, rest spots, trash cans, worship areas, and different

Pilgrim's Route Gratitude Open Chapel

Pilgrim's Route Mesa Colorada Hermitage

viewpoints while staying true to the existing topography. The two structures that your studio was responsible for were the Gratitude Open Chapel and the Mesa Colorada Hermitage. The chapel acts as a starting point of the route, with travelers using the walls to post why they are grateful and why they travel the route. The hermitage is the initial hermitage that people experience on the route. The structure is two walls folding into each other with a crack open to the sky, and these walls can serve as benches or an enclosed shelter that can be used as worship space or areas of rest.

Both elements are composed of simple geometries that create experiences through sunlight and openness. There's a lot of consideration and respect for the act of remembrance and memory. I imagine this comes through engagement and conversation with the users.
Casa Marbel came about after a devastating earthquake. Most

Casa Marbel

housing in Mexico is self-built, and many were in need of assistance following the disaster. The house is located at the foot of a sanctuary, which is a very respected area. The main goal here was to preserve the existing trees on the property, which act as the family's main source of income with the owners creating and selling crowns produced by the flowers that bloom on the tree. The other factor was to create a trio of sectors in the house that link the living spaces to the trees.

These projects represent a real dedication to listening to the constituents of a project. When did you start designing with the ethos of collaboration and listening that you have now? What started that for you?

BILBAO: It's a long answer. When I finished school and went into the professional world, I was really scared because I felt that I had learned nothing. I thought that I didn't take advantage of school enough and that it had been rushed. I don't know how in the world I was even able to graduate. I was like, "I don't know how to design anything." It was a very big insecurity. I saw all my peers very confidently designing things. So, I just started by saying, "Well, why don't we do this together?" Because then I could learn how to do it. After time, I realized that what I thought was insecurity was a discomfort with how I had learned architecture.

In architecture, I was taught to think that I had the tools to design anything. But I didn't think I had any tools to design anything, especially not for anybody else. Then I understood that I don't think anybody has the tools or the right to design anything for anybody else. When I started working collectively, I understood that there was a possibility of sharing different ways of approaching things. At least then there were different visions on the table. All the projects became a combination of thoughts by a combination of people, and the aim has always been to produce space with everyone that will inhabit it.

To arrive at the thought that, as individual architects, we should not have the right to design anything for anybody else took me twenty years. It is something I arrived at recently. At the beginning when I was doing this collective form of making, my first thought was, "I don't know anything, so let's do it collectively because I think that we can share knowledge." Then I thought, "Well, this is good because it opens up possibilities around thinking differently." I think it means that you respond a little bit more to the diverse population that will use these things.

But then I realized that what I was doing was not actually building. This is when I understood that there is a necessity to unpack all of the ways in which we see things through personal filters. We need to engage with all of the ways we might try to see the world through the eyes of others. We need to think about how we could engage in designing the world collectively. How can architecture, which I believe is always a collective act, be *made* as a collective act?

What happened with Casa Marbel? The caption or project description might say that we designed it, but I didn't design those houses. The people designed them. We were only there to help them realize their homes in specific ways. Physically, the houses failed after the earthquake, and people needed help in that way. When Mexico signed a trade agreement with the United States and Canada a number of years ago, a huge amount of cheap industrialized materials started to arrive to rural areas in Mexico where they never had been used before. Cinder blocks and cement and steel arrived in towns where people used to build with traditional materials and traditional methods of construction. This was all new to them.

Normally, local building methods were based on earth bricks, compressed earth, wood, wood sticks, palms, and other different things. Mostly they built with what was available regionally. The houses that failed were the result of a combination of the aspiration of modernity and the arrival of these unfamiliar supplies that came with it. This was exactly the moment that media started to penetrate everywhere. Media has promoted a specific way of living, such as the American dreamhouse being how the rest of the world wants to live, and this includes the idea that industrialized materials are what provides safety and security and—much more importantly—cultural belonging.

One of the issues is that those materials didn't arrive with any knowledge related to how to use them. People didn't know how to build with these materials. And this is why the earthquake in 2017 took down 500,000 houses. These houses failed because they were poorly built with these new materials. For example, in one town we discovered that rumors had spread about creating a rooted foundation slab by joining it with steel bars to the ground. But they didn't connect steel bars to the cinder blocks of the walls. They thought that rooting it to the ground was enough. When there was seismic movement, all of the walls collapsed because they were not anchored to the slab, they were just inserted onto it. We might think this is ignorant, but when materials show up with no instructions or know-how, you're just guessing at what is supposed to go where.

We had seen people trying to do things like this before, and we tried to warn them by talking about a better way to do it, but sometimes we would just get, "In your town you might build like that, but in our town, we build like this." And I said, "Okay, but let me tell you the logic of it." And then they would say, "Well, you might be right, but my neighbor taught me how to do this. And my neighbor is here and he's my neighbor, and you're never here. So, I'll do it the way he taught me, thanks." In the end, it's really a case of recognizing that it is their house, and they have the right to do as they wish. People have to be willing to learn or to be taught or to be helped.

So, we decided to work on that. First of all, we wanted to go back and rescue—so that they could rescue themselves—the local methods of construction. By then, nobody wanted it. This is because we as a society have been telling them in many ways that the future looks a particular way and success looks a particular way. When you have a house that looks like an American house, has a pitched roof, and is built with industrialized material, that is how to live properly. That's how we depict it everywhere. Media, books, films, you name it. Now we were back telling them, "No, you know what? It's better that you build in your own traditional methods." And they simply say, "No thanks."

Even in Mexico, the census classifies a place to live as precarious if it's not built with industrialized materials. When you fill out the census, you are literally marked as poor if your house is built with earth. So, people don't want to build with earth. In this case, we weren't able to convince them to rebuild theses house using earth. We told them that they would be able to build more space because those materials are local. They could build them with their neighbors. But, no. That's poor. And then we understood that they wanted to rebuild their town in a different way, and we should be able to provide them with better possibilities. We advised on how to use bricks to create foundations that are stable and that allow for their houses to be secure. But we didn't design a thing. They designed their houses. They built them. We just gave advice.

For example, there was one house in that town on the corner of a busy street. The family thought it was the busiest intersection around, though we didn't think it was that bad. They really didn't want their house to have windows that opened to the streets. We tried arguing that they were necessary for ventilation and illumination. In the end, they said, "We're not going to put windows." We were going to ask, "But how are you going to illuminate and ventilate?" And then we thought, "It's their house. They want to live that way. We should not impose."

JONES: They wanted privacy and quiet.

BILBAO: Whatever their reasons, they were *their* reasons, and they were going to build *their* house. If we were to design that house and put a window in, they would have completely sealed it up. Sometimes there are just things that you or I cannot understand. I cannot understand why someone would live like that, and they cannot understand why I would do something else. That is the moment where you realize you cannot be the other. So, again, what do we do? Maybe we become a tool for them to make whatever they want to, and we help them in whatever way we can to make it better, but not to impose the way that we think it should be. I'm always changing my vision and understanding that I cannot become the other. How can I enable an architecture that allows others to create their own living?

JONES: If you were to approach that situation again and go in from the starting point, recognizing and knowing what you know now, how would you approach the project?

BILBAO: I would be much more insistent and not give in so easily on the traditional materials. I would involve the people who had knowledge of building locally. I went back last year, and it was very sad. I sat with one of the families we had previously talked with and the father started crying. He said, "I regret so much that I didn't listen to you because this house is hell. It's too hot in the summers and it's too cold in the winters. Our old house with earth was really a refuge." I almost cried as well. It's very sad to see this process because it's rooted in a foreign idea and an imposition on how people should live regardless of where they are from.

Cinder block is a material that is cheap. But it requires layers to perform well in terms of structure, sound, and thermal behavior. It needs a lot of things. It's not simply a brick substitute. The earth doesn't need anything else. It's soundproof, and it's a temperature-regulating material. It's structural if it's well thought out. It's not a one-to-one swap, but that was an assumption that some people worked with.

JONES: Imagine yourself working for the Bureau of Indian Affairs and you're going to help the Navajo population with housing in a community where they've been underhoused and they've lost their homes to a variety of things. You go to a place where they've lived in a particular way for centuries and generations. Instead of considering options and having a discussion, the United States government delivers a bunch of concrete block and the next thing you know, your buildings are all lined up in military fashion regardless of the shape of the landscape, right? It's completely foreign.

BILBAO: This happens everywhere in the world.

JONES: Why don't we listen and engage in a dialogue with people who know their climate and who know their environment?

BILBAO: This is the adherence to and imposition of systems. This is the imperialism we live in. Once you build and sell this house that is not sustainable and that does not respond to its environment, you need to install air conditioning. You need to install all these systems that consume and produce what the system—the capitalist system—needs to exist. I'm not saying we should go back and live in tribes with teepees, but I do think there's something between these two extremes. The whole population is much healthier in general because of the advances we have made. Many buildings really do protect us from the environment in a way that is almost universally good.

Taken to an extreme, which is happening in many places and especially in the United States, architecture is starting to create a limit between our bodies and the ecosystem to such an extent that we are starting to disadapt from it. Many people live in 72-degree weather their whole lives. They're born in a place that is conditioned to 72 degrees. They go to a school that is again artificially conditioned to 72 degrees. The supermarket is 72 degrees. They're back again at their house and it's 72 degrees. Office, university, and everything else is at 72 degrees. This is regardless of the weather outside. When exposed to the weather for a number of hours, they're sick because the body has no idea how to cope with it. Architecture is at least partially responsible for how the human body relates to its environment in a healthy or unhealthy way.

STUDENT: If we can go back to Housing+ for a moment. One account says that you surveyed some 2,000 people and ran interviews with them asking, "What kind of housing would actually serve you?" Overwhelmingly, the response was something that looked like a traditional American or European-style house with a gable roof. How do you process that within the studio?

BILBAO: We were asked to design a model for government housing that provides for the people most in need. In Mexico, housing is a constitutional right. There are several programs in the government to make this right possible for the majority...in theory.

Housing is then fulfilled by different institutions in different ways. The program that fulfills the majority of the houses is not necessarily for the majority of the population because it's only for people that have a formal job. A formal job means a job that hires them with benefits within the law. This is when they're able to get a house that is financed by the economy. This is 40 percent of the population. Meanwhile, 60 percent of people have informal jobs. There are other programs who treat that 60 percent, and the one that we were working with is one of them. How it works in this system is that people go to these institutions and say, "I don't have the money and I need help to build my house." Then these institutions give you a manual of houses that you can choose from to be built on your plot. This was the program we were part of. Our design strategy was meant to be like that, with multiple different houses. Our design was also meant to be self-built, because it needs to be. It's one of the things that these houses need to work, and it needs to cost no more than $8,000 to build. An interesting story here is that we thought flat roofs were essential for this project because then the houses could be expanded and extended upward when warranted. When we did interviews, we found out that flat roofs, for them, meant that a project was unfinished. They wanted the pitched roof. Not because a pitched roof is an ideal or dream house, but because, when NAFTA poured materials into communities and they built with these materials and were not able to complete the dream, they left the houses unfinished with rebar sticking out waiting for construction to continue. It was originally seen as a gesture of progress, of the future, or of hope. But no one ever came to finish or expand, so the exposed rebar on a flat surface became a sign of failure. The pitched roof was a sign of completion and success.

STUDENT: We've already discussed Minimum Housing for Ocoyoacac a little bit. It's an arrangement of separate volumes around an open courtyard that ties together the private and communal spaces. Growth is cultivated through additional modules of single-family spaces arranged in a field around these courtyards. Population growth can continue to rise while maintaining relationships that are already accustomed to the culture in which the project is located. With that being said, how is the module an expression of generosity, cooperation, and listening?

BILBAO: One of the things I realized is that a module is an imposition of a way of living that doesn't completely allow for particular ways of being. I think the problem is really the necessity for the standardization of things. Maybe it's cheaper to buy a water closet than it is to create a dry bathroom, but then they buy a water closet and how do they use it with no sewage network? It is exactly that kind of problem. I think we realized that our design strategy was a failed idea in some ways and that these types of module houses could really only provide a solution in a very urban context—one that's connected to a grid. Maybe they don't work in rural areas. That's when we realized that our idea was not so well thought out. Thinking outside of the ideals of Western culture is hard.

It's the same with the hammocks. There are people who still are scandalized by someone sleeping in a hammock. Really? Why? Why do we have that concern? It's a luxury to live in a hammock in this place. I've been there so many times and I can't sleep in a hammock because I'm not used to it. Maybe it's my idea of physical normalcy or whatever. But I wish I could because that's the best way you can sleep in this weather. You don't need air conditioning here if you do that and that's exactly the point. Westerners often say, "Oh they cannot buy a bed, so let's help them buy a bed by bringing in donations." They don't need beds! That's my point with all of this. I have become aware of all these things and I need to consciously and unconsciously rethink my positions. It's real work to do that.

JONES: What I'm struck by is the way you've chosen to be in the community and how much time it's taken you to do so. You're there with an enormous sense of responsibility, and you recognize that you can't meet responsibilities in the way we've come to expect. Over an entire career you've absorbed and thought about this, and you've amended your values. I mean, you're just starting, right? So how many more transitions will you have to make? How many times are you going to have to check and challenge all the things you've learned in school? All of the things that you take for granted? All the things you think you know? Especially if you endeavor to work in a place that's not rooted in those things? Most of us never really leave our cultural values. How often is it that you're asked to practice in a place where you really have to learn? How often do we question these things daily? You're asking the hardest question that we have as architects.

BILBAO: I think that we need to think about that every day, and we need to question it every day. And that's what you said, "How do you keep questioning it every day?" I think one of the aspects that allows me to do that is I've always been very harsh on myself and I question everything that I do. Every time I go out and look at my own work, I say, "Well, I could have done it like this" and my husband says, "Tatiana, you did it very well!" And I'm like, "No, because I could have done—" and he says, "But you're too hard on yourself." One day I really reflected on that, and I thought that maybe I am too hard on myself. But it allows me to become very aware of the things around me, of what I do and what I see. Sometimes it gives me opportunities to grow. Sometimes it gives me opportunities to critique. I think that by questioning everything, we allow ourselves to be open. If we just follow the norms, I don't think we'll be as open to change.

JONES: After all, we have to keep our therapists employed.

BILBAO: Because they need money to survive. Therapists and architects need money for food as well.

STUDENT: Can you talk about your role as a woman in the discipline?

BILBAO: I was asked to give a lecture around the International Women's Day celebration in 2020, three days before COVID became fully present. I was invited to a conference that was held in Oaxaca, and I asked them what I should talk about. They said

Inner courtyard of the Sargfabrik (Vienna)

to just talk about my work, and so I decided to present my work within the context of how it has opened channels for women and how it has eased or erased discrimination. I had a long plane ride that gave me time to think and, when I started to put the lecture together, I understood that there was nothing in my work to advance the erasure of discrimination, but a lot to perpetrate the discrimination already in place.

I also realized that my architecture had nothing to do with advancing anything in terms of women's rights. I then presented my work by explaining which parts had failed to advance equal access to anything. I declared myself guilty, and then I declared myself also responsible to not do it again. At that point, I started to become much more conscious of everything, and I started thinking of the concept of the house. I mean, yes, we had already started thinking a lot about the house as a reproductive place. And yes, we had explored Ways of Life and the Solo House and Housing+ and these were driven by different ways of living and different types of cultures and different communities. But they were not addressing the other issues. For me, making social housing is about responding to a system that perpetuates exploitation and discrimination. It is the response to fix things related to very systemic problems. I think we have to tackle ways of making systemic change. This is why I think we must consider the making of cities that are surrendered to care and not production. There are some small-scale models for this that are worth considering.

There's another beautiful example in Vienna. It's called The Sargfabrik. It used to be a coffin factory, and they kept the name. It is a building that was repurposed in the 90s by a cooperative and the architect was among the cooperative. They set up the land as a seventy-one-unit building and it's really amazing. It's incredible architecture with these communal spaces. One is a public bath with different types of pools. It has a large pool, it has a small pool, it has a sauna, and so on. They're incredible. They have gardens, edible gardens, childcare, laundry, a kitchen that serves the community, and an auditorium that holds performances. It's seventy-one households in different arrangements. They have one unit where they can sleep twelve people individually and they use it for refugees. There are sometimes students there and it's great for students. I would live in this place for sure. They currently have 1,500 requests for people who want to live there. It works perfectly well. I met one of the original cooperative founders, and they told me something really important when we were talking about capitalism. They said, "This is not a democracy. You know, everybody now tends to think that it's a democracy but it's not, because a democratic system is based on majority rules. That doesn't necessarily include everybody, right? Here we include everybody." So, it's not a democracy. How does it work? She said, "Every decision is unanimous." I was like, "Really?"

JONES: It's sociocratic. I worked for a pro-housing community here in Columbus that was made up of maybe seven families and another ten trying to get in. They're still trying to form, and every decision is supposed to be sociocratic. It's really hard to do.

BILBAO: I wanted her to describe the manner in which they work, and I asked her, "Does everybody vote yes or no and that's it?" She said, "No, obviously not. We don't agree on anything!" (laughter) She said, "Unanimity comes when we all agree consciously and outwardly and then that is the decision we go with. Even if you inwardly agree or not." Eventually, in order to move forward, you need to vote to move forward, even if you are reluctant. This requires sharing your own thoughts and listening to those of others. People who were against any decision that was going to be made needed to express why they were against it. Everybody needed to listen as to why they were against it, and everybody needed to be conscious of the fact that they were against something and why they were against it. She said that this made individuals conscious and aware of the issues and that topics and decisions could be raised in the community knowing that participants would be more careful to understand those issues. This way everyone is considered.

JONES: It's an enormous investment of time. Being aware or informed is incredibly demanding.

BILBAO: They said that it took them three days of discussion to resolve a color issue related to painting the facade, so imagine how much time other things may take. (laughter) But that is one of the things that made me realize why we create a system where we don't have to do that. We avoid these things and have architects and developers who decide the color of the facade. We live in a system that now needs you to have time to work and not have time to allow you to solve conflicts that build communities. What happened? I asked them what the result of their system was. She said, "It takes us three days to buy a coffee machine, but then we're all content with the coffee machine. Trust is built. Subsequent decisions get easier and easier because you trust each other. Once you know you've been heard—even if someone doesn't agree with you—you know they heard you." That's the community part of it. It doesn't happen overnight. It is an investment of time.

SOCIAL LANDSCAPES + HOUSING AND DWELLING

STUDENT: Your website places your projects into six different categories: density, social landscape, education, affordability, domesticity, and culture. These are presented without definitions. Some of the categories are easy to define while others are more vague or suggestive. You have described your own work as, "A totality of context," and, "The sum of the site, geography, economics, politics, society, history, and culture, whether visible or invisible in a place." This is similar to what Stan Allen describes as *field conditions*, which are, "any formal or spatial matrix capable of unifying diverse elements while respecting the identity of each." This results in a configuration of porous aggregated assemblies that, through their loose connections, create local interconnectivity. Therefore, projects placed under the *Social Landscape* category might be described as those that foster new or strengthening social relationships between users by way of responsive or flexible field conditions.

Staterra partial plan

Staterra is a good example. It's a compound of diverse programs, all to do with short-term stays, hotel-like rooms, villas, or simple stays with some amenities, and a services area. The project is organized around an overlay of systems, with the hotel rooms confined to a central area and organized around the intersection of rectangles and circles. This generates a change of material and a hybrid volume, which in turn begins to disassemble the rigidity of the rectangle and open it up to the exterior. While privacy is a factor, the circles produce axial relationships with the surrounding rooms to promote a social interactive and interstitial space between them. The landscape itself begins to form relationships through material changes tangentially touching circles spread out over the site. When multiple villas are situated on the same circle, there is an implied idea of coexistence and sharing. Whether relationships here come to fruition is up to the user, but the spatial organization welcomes overlap via these boundaries. Where most circles are occupied by one, two, or four villas, the entirety of the hotel rooms are located within one larger circle. It's landscape that's meant to be social.

The Minimum Housing for Ocoyoacac project is categorized under affordability, which is appropriate because the material and the pavilionization of the project makes this possible. But the expandability of the courtyard between pavilions creates a unified field that strengthens ideas of a connected network of inhabitants. Spaces surrounding the houses act as non-descript points of congregation and interaction. Materiality, affordability, flexibility, and expandability become equally influential fields that together make the project whole.

Some of the work that falls under educational work is also designed under similar understandings of the field and, I would argue, with the social landscape in mind. Estoa—UDEM is at the University

Estoa—UDEM section collage

of Monterrey and serves as the main entrance of the university. It also works as a link between city, campus, and the people, blurring lines between the rigid limit that previously existed between the city and university, and the landscape and the built campus.

Collegium is an ongoing project in Arévalo, Ávila, Spain. It's an institution inserted within an historic context. The plan is based on the Jesuit complex of Arévalo during the sixteenth and seventeenth centuries while the exhibits are dispersed in a vertical field and vary in scale as a way to mitigate obstruction to the existing fabric.

These larger, educational projects speak to their situational relationships and the networks of fields that they respond to as much as many of the other projects in order to make new interactions between their university constituents and their larger contexts. On some level, I wonder if the separation of projects into six categories (on the website) does a disservice to them by restricting them to a singular identity?

A website has to work with respect to organization, navigation, and aesthetics. It also must work for different types of visitors, which we might describe as those knowing what they're looking for and those who don't. But a site can also be a catalog. Aesthetically, the site makes clear the design values of the firm. The site is clear and straightforward aesthetically. My question has to do with the organization of the projects into their discreet categories. I would guess that the project index is targeted towards the user who knows what they're looking for, and that the city map is targeted toward those who don't. Both manners of organization have their benefits, but the project index siloes the projects into a singular identity while the city map does the work of suggesting the interconnected values between the work.

I'm interested to hear your view on how things are arranged on the website and what purpose this arrangement serves for you. Maybe it's getting into the weeds a bit in terms of definitions and their value, but I'm wondering if you can elaborate on this issue?

BILBAO: This is a key question, and I appreciate that you posed it. I have always had a hard time thinking of the website. It was a long time before we had one, and this is actually kind of recent. One of the reasons why I've always had some doubts about how to do one well was that you need a way to archive the projects, and this ends up classifying them, and I have always refused typical categories in many ways. The second thing is that I have always seen the internet as a very dynamic interface, and I feel that webpages should be interactive and progressive, changing, and constantly updated, but we don't have time or energy for that; it's a whole other project and field of design. I very much like your assessment, though. We really struggled to find the correct label for each project since we like to think that they can be seen and hopefully used in many ways. This would mean that they would need to be categorized in many forms, and that is the problem of categorization; we tend to think that such categories are determined and fixed.

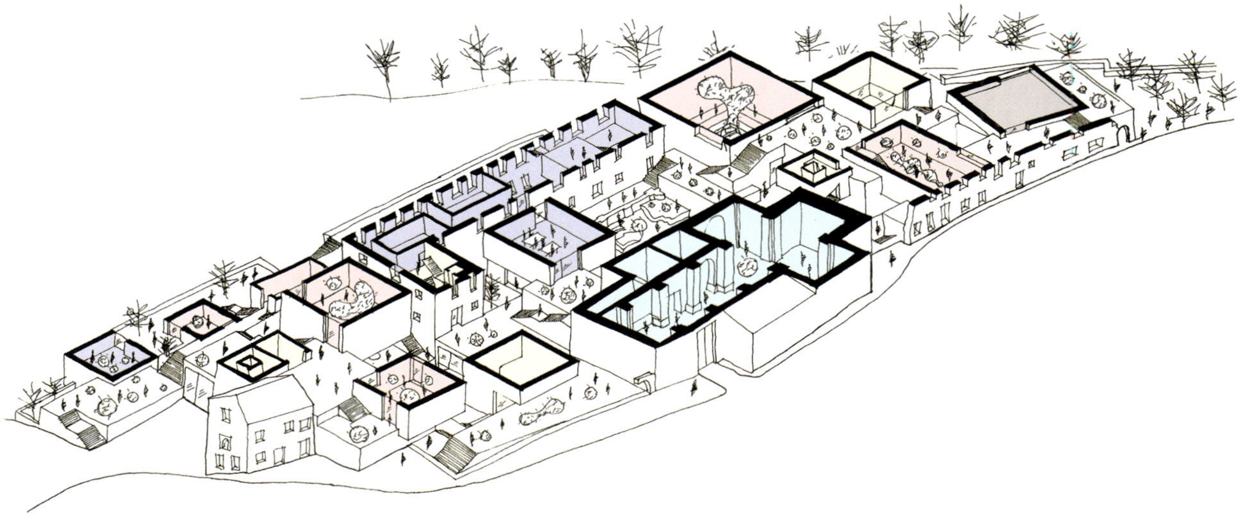

Collegium plan illustration

JONES: With respect to Staterra, can you discuss the geometry that you used? The circle is an abstraction that scales up or down. I think it's being used as a scalar device to measure and define space and then incorporate the idea of *commoning* into it. You're looking at land, cities, and planning here, so it's really an abstraction. It's not rooted in the place per se, because culture is always the root. I think scale is one of the things that we do most poorly in architectural education. We're constantly looking at things in a pretty abstract way, and we really forget about size, scale, and what those things mean. I really like this as a way to organize a project.

BILBAO: We were definitely considering scale and the relationship to the ground with all of the projects that are mentioned here. It's about how to guide the scale and how to relate to the ground in this specific place—on this specific piece of land. These projects are all very different places. In the case of Staterra, it's related to creating more density. It's been a very tough, long process. We've been working on this for eight years. Many phases have happened already. One day they said, "Thank you for your work, but we're not going to do this. We're going to sell or lease the land to a hotel chain, and they have their own architects." We were completely demoralized. After that they called back, and they wanted a completely different idea; they wanted a more loosely knit community and, for us, imagining that was hard because the project is not just about developing land; it's about developing new kinds of space while thinking about and challenging the definitions that we assume to be true.

STUDENT: Maybe this is a good segue to discussing housing specifically. You have said, "Everything around the house is part of the house and, likewise, the unit itself functions within a much larger environment." This statement remains the core of your studio's design philosophy with respect to housing, whether it's social housing or high-end single-family homes. This is in contrast to an understanding of housing in the United States, where the typical home is inwardly focused and rooted in a history of the nuclear family and the ideology of the division of domestic labor. I'm wondering if we can speculate on the very definition of housing, its components, and its features within a world that is clearly facing multiple crises.

Merriam-Webster's definitions for housing, dwelling, and domesticity are pretty basic and lack nuance. Notably, there's some distinction between *housing as a shelter* and *housing as a dwelling*. I would argue that a house becomes a dwelling once it's been lived in, cared for, and has begun to accumulate identity and memories from those who live there. Most of us are familiar with the concept of Maslow's hierarchy of needs, the most basic of which are shelter, food, warmth, and security. These are the foundations for proper human development. It seems obvious, but adequate housing is at the heart of influencing who we are or can become.

The earliest housing wasn't much more than nests and primitive shelters but were clearly aimed at manipulating the environment for some advantage. Caves were used as shelters, but also as a

Los Terrenos

dwelling shared by multiple generations. Dwellings allowed cultural knowledge to be passed on via cave paintings, storytelling, tool making, cooking, and burials. Mud brick houses are known to have existed as far back as 9000 BCE and en masse at Catal Huyuk as far back as 7500 BCE. The infrastructural systems differed vastly, but these were communal living scenarios. The Greek megaron is a model on which the classical tradition built and is perhaps the true ancestor of the American home. The megaron over time split into the *andron* and *gynaikos*, flanking or abutting a communal space where collective family activity took place and guests were received. Architecture begins responding to work based on gender, and this is a major development for housing in the Western world. In the Roman domus, the nature of this separation is enhanced by an even more patriarchal society. The service spaces are shoved to the back of the house, forcing the kitchen and places of domesticity out of sight. The head of household would likely be engaged in business at the front of the home, which is still accessible to the public, but now there's distance between family and community functions of the home.

If we take the big leap to the twentieth century, the nuclear family of contemporary United States culture is made for a strictly defined group of people living a prescribed ideal lifestyle who are sheltered from their neighbors and far from town centers.

Architecture defines housing as a sheltered living space designed to house either a collective group or an individual, primarily as a zone of personalized habitation. Your studio defines housing as a built extension of the surrounding environment that's designed to provide spaces for close knit occupant interactions. You consider housing a human right while seeking to define housing beyond simple shelter. These housing projects are always related to the scale of an individual working with the limits and problems of what they're faced with at any given site. Your work also tries to foster a connection to the site, which includes the individual and collective experiences that can emerge there.

Housing+ is affordable housing. The primary ambition of the

Productive House by Fernanda Canales

Bruma House by Fernanda Canales + Claudia Rodriguez

design is to consider occupants and future inhabitants as those who dictate the form and function. Silica II – Robles 700 is a large-scale housing project. The living unit is at the center of the adjacent configurable social spaces. Los Terrenos is designed to merge with its surroundings by way of materiality such as windows and mirrors. It facilitates a relationship to place but is not solely focused on the inhabitants themselves. So, there are a number of ways that you approach the idea of dwelling.

Fernanda Canales did a house for the MOS master plan as part of the Minimum Housing for Ocoyoacac project. It is a single-family dwelling formed by a modular volume of thirty-five square meters. It is adaptable and can grow along with a family via the addition of more modules articulated through a series of patios. The patios themselves can vary in size based on the desired proximity to the modular framework. The first module includes the following: kitchen, bathroom, living room, and dining all on the ground floor with a bedroom on the platform above. The second module would include more bedrooms and other bathrooms as well as more flexible spaces such as studios and workshops. With all this said, the program here can be altered and oriented to suit local traditions and cultures. For example, a kitchen can be oriented outward towards the patio and the community to promote communal cooking and eating. Canales' Bruma House explodes the housing program into separate blocks centered around a patio, questioning the Western archetype of the house as single contained thing. Each piece of the program has autonomy but works as a singular unit due to the central patio and a unified material choice of painted concrete. During the initial design phase, questions arose as to what to do about the trees. The result was a minimal impact to existing forest, thus leading to a rotation of blocks. The nine rotating blocks are interconnected through a series of established views and smaller landscapes.
There are clearly shared ambitions between your work and other work that is happening right now. Your projects consider a number of things: the geographical and environmental features of the location, the potential for communal space that can be made, the larger cultural context that the project may inherit. In your work there's a real interest in leaving it up to the inhabitants to interpret what these spaces could become and how to use them. Do you think these projects address the climate crisis? Do you think these projects have potential in scenarios of disaster...where we perhaps have a massive number of people who need to be relocated?

BILBAO: There are a number of issues that you raise here. Both Housing+ and Minimum Housing for Ocoyoacac are design strategies that are modular. They're not ready-made but they are rapidly produced. These are two models: one is for a more rural context, and the other one is a little bit more suburban. I think that because they are easy and cheap to build, they're meant to work for certain situations. I think they investigate the problem of making homes and shelters for people, but they're not meant to be shelters in an emergency situation. They're just homes for people that are available, adaptable, easy, and cheap to build. I don't think that they explicitly address anything that has to do with the climate crisis. If they were meant to do that in a focused way, I would say that our response would need to be something much more durable and much more rooted in the place, because if you're going to spend money on material, it should be for something that is more permanent. These projects are not done with any type of recycled material, either. We could consider them to be capable as displacement housing I suppose, since they can be built cheaply and easily anywhere. So, I would say that anyone who has been displaced from the world in some manner or from conditions of privilege that wants to use these houses should have access to the plans. They're built and inhabited in incredibly difficult conditions, so these houses become better solutions than what is on the ground in almost every case. But I would critique my own project by saying that they don't address community as well as they could. They're not rooted in the local communities because they're not done locally. They're not rooted in specific people or in material. They are prototypes that, to some degree, are considered broadly applicable to various environments or places. As such, the specificity that is needed to connect to a particular place is less present.

That said, with respect to some of your definitions or comparisons, our modules are not intended to have any specific program, yet you're analyzing them through programmatic definitions. Those definitions—all of them—are programmatically driven. Our modules are meant to be used for anything. There are different sizes, but every module could be used for whatever the occupant wants.

I also think it's a bit unfair to compare some projects. You mention our Los Terrenos and Canales' Casa Bruma. Those projects can be compared because they are high-end houses. But I don't know if I like to compare these projects to some of the others. I understand that in some way we have to couch projects under a particular definition or category, and of course we are dealing with issues of dwelling and housing in all of these cases, but we are also working with different populations that have different needs and desires. I'm not saying anything is categorically wrong with how you're thinking about it, but I think that the attempt at comparison goes a bit too far in some cases. I like the idea that we can compare things because of arrangement, but this is a very particular mode of critique and abstracts away some very important elements related to the context and the user and I think this is unfair. Projects are more than formal relationships.

STUDENT: I think the comparisons were meant to get a particular idea on the table, which is that the overall economy of a house or dwelling is part of the consideration of building.

BILBAO: I agree. I believe completely that the same operations are considered with almost any project that deals with housing or dwelling. Use of patterns, context, responsibility in the use of materials. We carry these concerns with us with every project, as do others. The responsibility of the use of scale, the use of space, and how to acknowledge the site is present regardless of how much budget we have. I simply think it's hard to compare some of these projects. Even within categories or typologies, there's a range of subcategories or subtypes.

STUDENT: With respect to COVID or other unforeseen pandemics, do you think that a communal approach to housing could accommodate the need for isolation?

BILBAO: I think we cannot be isolated again. It was an epidemic before COVID; it is worse now. We need each other to exist, and this means needing to be around each other. I think that the problem of the pandemic was not the shared community, but the non-communal type of living that has become prevalent, because this is when the threat became really difficult to control. It sounds contrary, but if we can make bubbles of sustained communities and you can isolate that community, it becomes a known population that can be protected easier. The majority of the population couldn't stay home during COVID. You have to remember that fact. The ability to stay home was a luxury for a very specific demographic of people. Many people could not simply acclimate themselves to merging work life with home life because they had to go out to work, to eat, to shop, or to care for others. There were a lot of people that had to figure out how to work from home, but there were many more people who had to confront the dangers and realities of having to continue to go out of the home in order to work.

JONES: Those who take care of others, such as nursing staff, doctors, and essential workers were and are vulnerable. They're the ones putting their lives at elevated risk.

BILBAO: Of course. People who prepare food, work electric lines, manage waste and internet, and other public services were critical for those staying home. These are the people that could not stay home. The privelaged population couldn't have stayed safe at home without them. This is the group of people that maintain and sustain life in many ways and that normally have the lower paying jobs and are not acknowledged. Have we learned to appreciate them enough now? For us, the part of the population that was able to stay home, which was about ten percent of the world, was a consideration, but it wasn't as big a consideration as those who could not stay home, which was 90 percent of the population. I think it's really odd to believe that we need to think of and build spaces of isolation. Safety and the popular well-being are critical, but I don't think it's possible because the majority has to be out of that situation in order for it to happen. I think we're seeing some of the fallout from lack of interaction and will continue to see it, especially in younger generations.

STUDENT: I think the single-family home is one of the culprits here. We've looked at the effects of the pandemic on suburban areas, and it's actually very damaging to the idea of community. It damaged almost every community, but there were particular forms of damage where single family homes exist en masse.

JONES: COVID taught us that. The pandemic taught us that. We have seen the cost of isolation because this scenario amplified it. Hopefully we learned something. What can we do with that?

BILBAO: If houses were a community of fifteen to twenty-five people making things happen for themselves, fewer people would have to be out there. We have to understand that living in communities will prevent future pandemics and protect the most vulnerable. As I said, it's the most privileged people who are more likely to have the least problems with COVID because we are healthy and have access to services. We have incredible healthcare around us. We are very nurtured. We can stay home so we're less exposed. But many people exposed themselves to risks because they had to. I actually think that a communal approach to living and housing will be protective and will help against future pandemics. I think that care could become a new lens through which we look at settlement patterns, dwellings, and market choices.

COLLABORATION

STUDENT: I understand that collaboration is at the heart of any profession, network, or relationship, and that it can be interpreted in many ways. Perhaps we can define it as the action of working with someone to produce or create something.

Looking at your work, I understand that collaboration is not only an act of working to create something together, but an outlook that can lead to a design process. One framework for understanding collaboration comes from the idea of commoning, which is defined by Stefan Gruber (assistant professor of architecture at Carnegie Mellon University and the curator of the exhibition *An Atlas of Commoning*) as, "the process of sharing and negotiating access for both material and immaterial resources." I would say that commoning is integral to how a design process is cultivated through collaborators. To collaborate, one must share resources with team members, engineers, organizations, and city officials. To design spaces of commoning, one must collaborate with users, neighborhoods, and communities. I think that there are different scales of collaboration, and I'd like to frame some of your work through these scales.

Some scales of collaboration consider operations within a small group—a studio perhaps—and accounts for the relationships between team members. At this scale of collaboration, there are several key contributors: designers, architects, project managers, engineers, and principles. We understand that there are certain hierarchies within each office and different techniques of management, workflow, and communication. Collaboration is needed because there's a constant sharing of resources and knowledge on all sides—it's not just the delegation of assignments. Teams need to have a degree of self-organization and the ability to share information while simultaneously handling a specific area of work.

It's clear that there's almost always an active collaboration between, for example, an engineer and an architect. I would argue that there's always greater potential in co-mingling coordination between diverse individuals with different training, backgrounds, worldviews, and demographics. From what I know about the layout of your studio through reading and watching interviews, it's clear that an open and collaborative process takes place within the office, and that relationships with other collaborators are used as a means to brainstorm ideas. It's clear that documentation of ongoing projects is constantly being posted around conference rooms, office tables, and boards as a way of allowing employees to easily share ideas without mitigating access to resources. I would say that this encourages an open network that facilitates an iterative process and emphasis on open team dynamics. I would call this commoning.

Other scales of collaboration happen between various communities or groups, sometimes simultaneously. Walk the Line is a joint realization between Rozana Montiel, Derek Dellekamp, Alejandro Hernández, your office, a community in Miravalle, Mexico, and an exhibition in the Venice Biennale, among others. I think collaboration can begin with internal research that happens within a group before a site is known or visited. This research becomes a position or philosophy on how to work. In this case, it's a mindset that is shared by your office and the client, and that seems really important. This community in Mexico was well organized, having secured grants and funding from numerous institutions. They understood that issues inside their community were problems that had to be solved together and as part of a larger effort. The mindset of each party here dovetails nicely into a working relationship that allows for you to work the way that you think is important. It really is an ideal scenario for the approach and methodologies that are present in your practice.

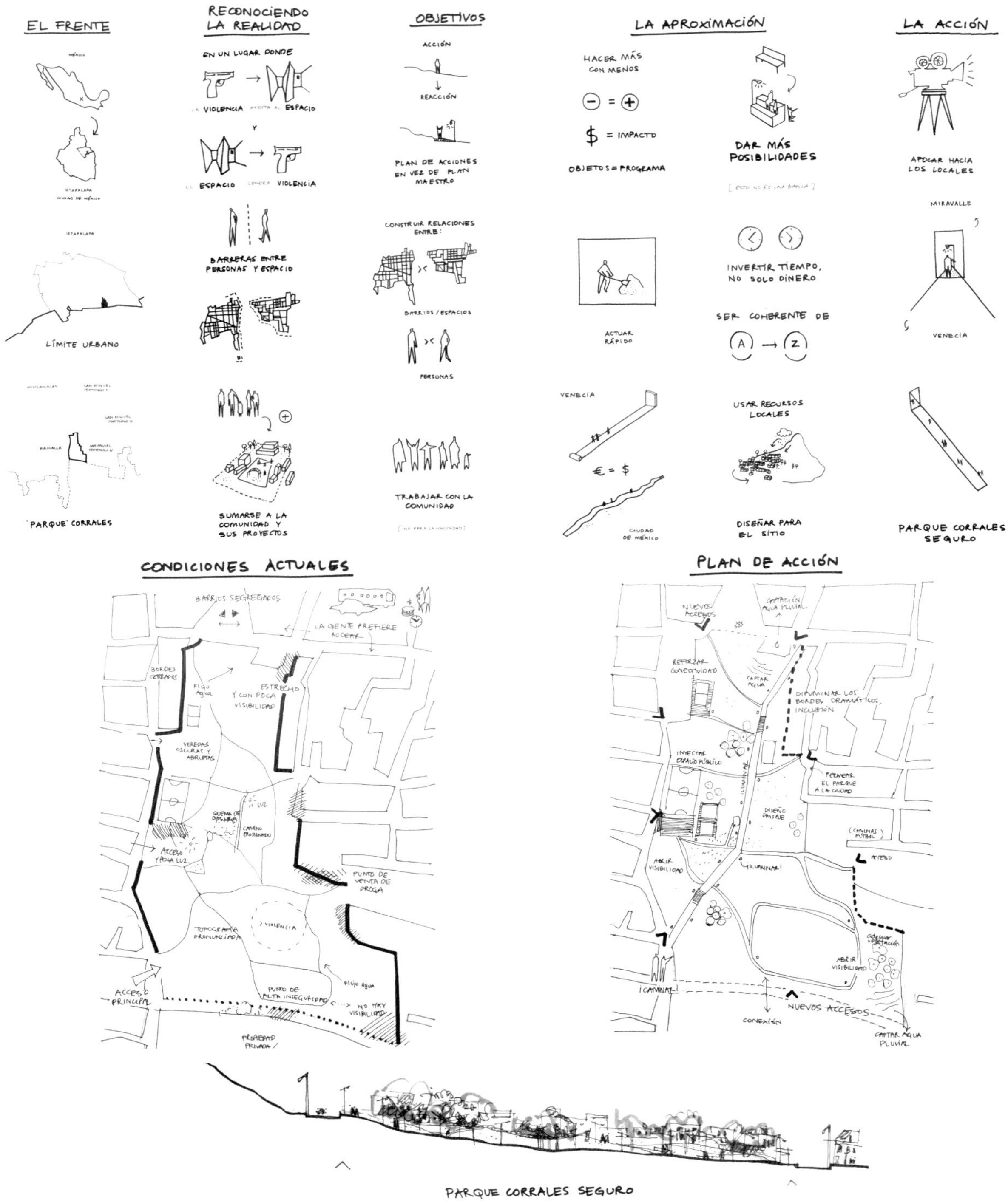

Diagrams and concepts of Walk the Line, Biennale di Venezia 2016

Once you are in the community and on-site physically, this scale of collaboration often seeks additional opportunities and collaborators. One external opportunity in this case is the Venice Biennale. The project is a unique chance to have the physical reality of the built work in Mexico represented in the Biennale, which would express a mode of working that isn't present in many practices. But there are other collaborators involved, too. There are those who can offer insight into areas you're unfamiliar with. Rozana Montiel, a Mexico City-based architect, knew the vernacular of the site and was also able to help further organize community outreach. Others worked on the exhibition in Venice and offered expertise in a gallery setting. These are project team members in a real sense, if not literally part of Tatiana Bilbao ESTUDIO.

Involving the community in the design process can include everything from informal interviews to jointly-developed sketches to meetings with various stakeholders. We think this process shows a few things to the community you're working with. First, it shows what is possible in terms of both collaboration and design, as well as things that, even in dire situations, can be accomplished. Something as simple as walking across the site together can instill some form of hope, but it also establishes a sense of ownership into the project for the community and helps to situate its future use and upkeep.

Larger-scale collaboration is needed to work across national borders. Your work is in numerous countries across the world. There are unfamiliar and diverse forms, policies, and practices that negate operating on certain assumptions. Collaborating is key to figuring out what is needed for a specific population, area, or moment. Projects that exist within master plans are especially applicable here, as there are often intimate timelines and relationships between projects that are being done by different offices. Your office has worked within the master plans of others and have invited others to work within the context of master plans that you've developed.

Sometimes larger-scale collaboration is defined by operations outside of the firm, city, and the country, and includes ideological principles that intend to influence design globally for the betterment of communities. A really good example is the National Memorial for Peace and Justice by MASS Design Group. The client in this case was Bryan Stevenson of the Equal Justice Initiative, who noticed that countries in Africa chose to acknowledge their turbulent past by confronting it in the form of national memorials. He proposed a similar project for the United States that would be the first national memorial dedicated to the more than 4,000 lives lost to lynching. MASS Design Group founder Michael Murphy found out about this and reached out to Stevenson, who in turn hired MASS Design Group for the project's design. The collaboration diagram for a project like this includes individuals, large companies, local businesses and organizations, institutional entities, landscape architects, other architecture firms, engineering firms, international artists, and so on. There are always a lot of consultants on almost any project, but it would seem like including the stakeholders on projects with ambitions like this means the collaboration has to be cohesive.

Ultimately, I understand collaboration as a means of recalibrating efforts to do things as guided by the rules of commoning at the local and global scales. With all of that being said, how do you personally collaborate within your office and how has your approach to collaboration grown or changed over time?

BILBAO: It's an interesting framework and a valuable way to think of the issues. I would add that there is collaboration and there is coordination, and they are different things. There are many times that we cannot necessarily collaborate and simply need to make decisions. Within the office, I do not do everything myself, so we need to coordinate decision-making processes. I think collaboration is what happens when you share things, and people are able to express themselves in a project. A project is a result of many ways of thinking and doing. I would say that I think that the truest form of collaboration is what you are referring to as the larger-scale collaborations.

The projects of Housing+ are very small houses in Mexico. They are truly collaborative all the way through the process, from the start to the end. Everyone has something that they have authorship over, though perhaps *authorship* isn't the right word. Everybody put their knowledge into the collective action required to build those houses. I think that, for me, that's an extra-large collaboration. It's not about the size of the project, and it's not about the distance from familiarity. It's truly about the number of people that were able to provide their input and knowledge to a project in order to help define it. Every project is thought up by someone yet has the collective knowledge of many to make it happen. Any project that is a final vision or thought that one person had is a small-scale project precisely because there are fewer people who contribute. With a lot of projects, there isn't an initial vision; the project literally emerges from conversations and research or communication between parties. Everyone involved all came together to form the ideas, gather the resources, develop the methods, and source the materials. If forced to define it, I would say that my understanding of collaboration exists around my scale of value, which is that each person is part of a whole. I think that our office has historically operated at a smaller scale of collaboration, but we want it to move consistently closer to the very large scale. I think that the project with the Venice Biennale is closer to a very large collaboration because we collaborated in many ways, at many stages, with so many people.

I might argue that Lyon is much closer to a small-scale collaboration or a fairly typical type of architectural coordination. The pilgrimage route would be a larger-scale collaboration for sure. We also have built two projects in China, and the collaboration and coordination that needs to happen there is very pronounced. You described it very well as an act of commoning. An act of commoning is when everybody has a stake in what happens. This is what I truly aspire to do.

JONES: Commoning gets in the way of some normal power structures. I think what strikes me when I hear you speak—and I like the way that collaboration is framed as either small-scale or large-scale—is your commitment to a mission. Your lifelong commitment as a practitioner is to go to a specific place and maximize your potential with a hyperawareness of the challenges along the way. It's the commitment that keeps the drive going.

BILBAO: I believe this is true. I think life is a collaborative act. We can't exist without the other. It's truly linked to our own nature, so I believe it's only the natural and necessary way of doing things. In terms of the built environment, the architect is only a small part of the collection of expertise. Everybody has a part in building, but we should put more attention into those who are finally going to inhabit what is built. Those individuals and groups should have a major role. One group will have the literal tools to make it, another group has the financial tools to fund it, and another group has the legal tools to get it approved within a larger ambition. Everyone should have a stake in what is happening, and everyone should have input.

REPRESENTATION

STUDENT: Representation is an important issue in your work. It is how we communicate to each other as architects, it's how we communicate to those who work with architects, and it's how we communicate with the public. We have standard (or conventional) languages in architecture, and we have alternate languages in architecture. Your use of collage is an important piece of how you communicate ideas to others.
Collage originally dates back to 200 BC in China, but I'd like to discuss your work in relation to cubism and Dadaism specifically. For the cubists, collage could be a reactionary tool to the world around them and it helped to explore possibilities related to illusion, three dimensionality, depth, and scale. In short, it potentially allows one to play with suggestion and ambiguity. Collage was useful in challenging the seriousness of high art at the time, and it allowed for varied interpretations.

Dadaism is primarily a reaction to World War I and incorporates elements of chaos, absurdity, and the nonsensical. We might say that Dadaism leaned into techniques such as photo montage and the use of imagery of figures that were known or understood. There are challenges to the status quo in each movement and, in each case, they're trying to reconsider those things that we think we understand.

Are your collages of environments meant to raise a critique in any way related to this? Are you inspired by any particular movement in art history that led to your current representation style?

BILBAO: I'm always influenced by history. My understanding of collage is that it is a medium to represent things, and sometimes there is an impossibility of representing something with a simple image. So perhaps that is the common thread? A collage is one image with the ability to incorporate a lot of layers within it. Both Dadaism and cubism appeared in revolutionary times and allowed new reactions to emerge. For me, collage allows for anyone's immersion in the representation in a way that no other technique does. You could ask anyone what a particular collage represents, and everybody would say something different. This is because we see these images with our own eyes, our own filters, and our own experience and perspective. Some might say they see the joy between crises while others would say they see the world falling apart. Some might say that something represents industrialization while others would say a collage shows social unrest. I'm just making up various possible reactions here, but I think that those are the possibilities of collage. I think that this is what architecture should be able to do. Architecture should allow anybody to identify themselves as part of it. This is why collage is important to us.

STUDENT: The Research Center of the Sea of Cortez would be good to discuss because it includes different methods of collage. Do you start with collage as a way of thinking about a

Research Center of the Sea of Cortez collage

Research Center of the Sea of Cortez illustraticn

project? Do you do it near the end? Are there different timelines and processes?

BILBAO: Let me begin by saying that I think we are a form of collage, individually and as an office. I think architecture is always a collage. I use collage in a more philosophical way at any point in the process of design and as a communication tool. The procees is never a linear one and it's also never a straightforward answer because every time is very different. Every project starts with conversations and an exchange of ideas through words. That's something that is fairly constant. When do the images emerge? It's very dependent on how well we can express those ideas and how quickly we can respond to them. The images are processes that emerge in order to be able to start shaping the architecture. Sometimes they are a very immediate response and sometimes they happen afterwards. Sometimes images that are done much later in the process represent our thoughts from the very beginning of the project. We sometimes make them by thinking back to the beginning conversations, but they're not necessarily done at the exact time that we sat down and brainstormed the ideas.

STUDENT: Have you ever looked back at a collage and modified it because of new discoveries or new realities?

BILBAO: We have certainly revised collages. We have thrown out many collages. (laughter) We have redone and copied collages. Someone asked us to do a replica of one once, and I was hesitant because I thought that it was a unique piece. But then we did it, and we changed things a bit, and I quite liked it.

STUDENT: You communicate through your collages to other architects, stakeholders, clients, and community members. Do you find them to be more responsive to the collages or more emotionally connected to the project when you choose this form of representation?

BILBAO: Yes, for sure. There are many more reactions, and they're more extreme reactions. There are people who hate what they see in the image and people who love what see in the image. There are reactions when you present finished documentation such as realistic renderings or plans or drawings, but they're mild reactions. "It's nice. It's okay." But then they see the collages, they say, "Are

Research Center of the Sea of Cortez collage

Research Center of the Sea of Cortez illustration

Research Center of the Sea of Cortez illustration

Research Center of the Sea of Cortez illustration

you crazy?" I think that those are the reactions I really want to have because this is when you are able to express and define and clarify ideas. Sometimes we use collages to provoke. We do that when the direction of the project is not quite going where we want or when we feel stuck.

On the other hand, we also do it to reinforce ideas. We're able to use certain types of representation to describe our vision. Sometimes they're like, "We've got it." And then we're able to push it. I really think that they provoke more reactions than any other type of conventional or familiar way of representing architecture. We could represent projects with typical drawings, but I think that this type of representation is very static and very scripted. I hope that by doing what we do, we open channels for those buildings not to be as static and to be part of a more fluid conversation. Do we mind that the collage is different than the built thing? No. I always say, "My goal is for people to interact with the building, not just with the space that the building forms." For example, if there's graffiti all over a project, I love it. People are like, "What? They graffitied your space!" Graffiti is people taking over a building. It's one form of what we want architecture to do and be now and in the future.

STUDENT: The idea of change over time is one thing that's hard to express in a single drawing. Do you always choose to tell a story about your buildings?

BILBAO: I taught a studio where I asked students to write a story about a group of people. They could write whatever story they wanted to, and people wrote completely different things. Then they designed their project after the story. But the first idea was to just write. No images, no anything.

JONES: They had to use words? Architects are terrified of words.

BILBAO: When words work against them. But architects are very accepting of words when it suits their purposes. I think we need to learn the value of words and stories as a way of creating spaces for those stories to really succeed and exist.

JONES: Are you optimistic? I think stories are where we have the potential to be optimistic. Of course, stories can lean the other way.

BILBAO: This building [Knowlton Hall] is a beautiful building that incorporates nature throughout. This is an environment that allows stories to unwind here. I have always thought that this is one of the most optimistic potentials of architecture. What is going to happen? What is going to remain when we are gone? What are the stories that will be made here?

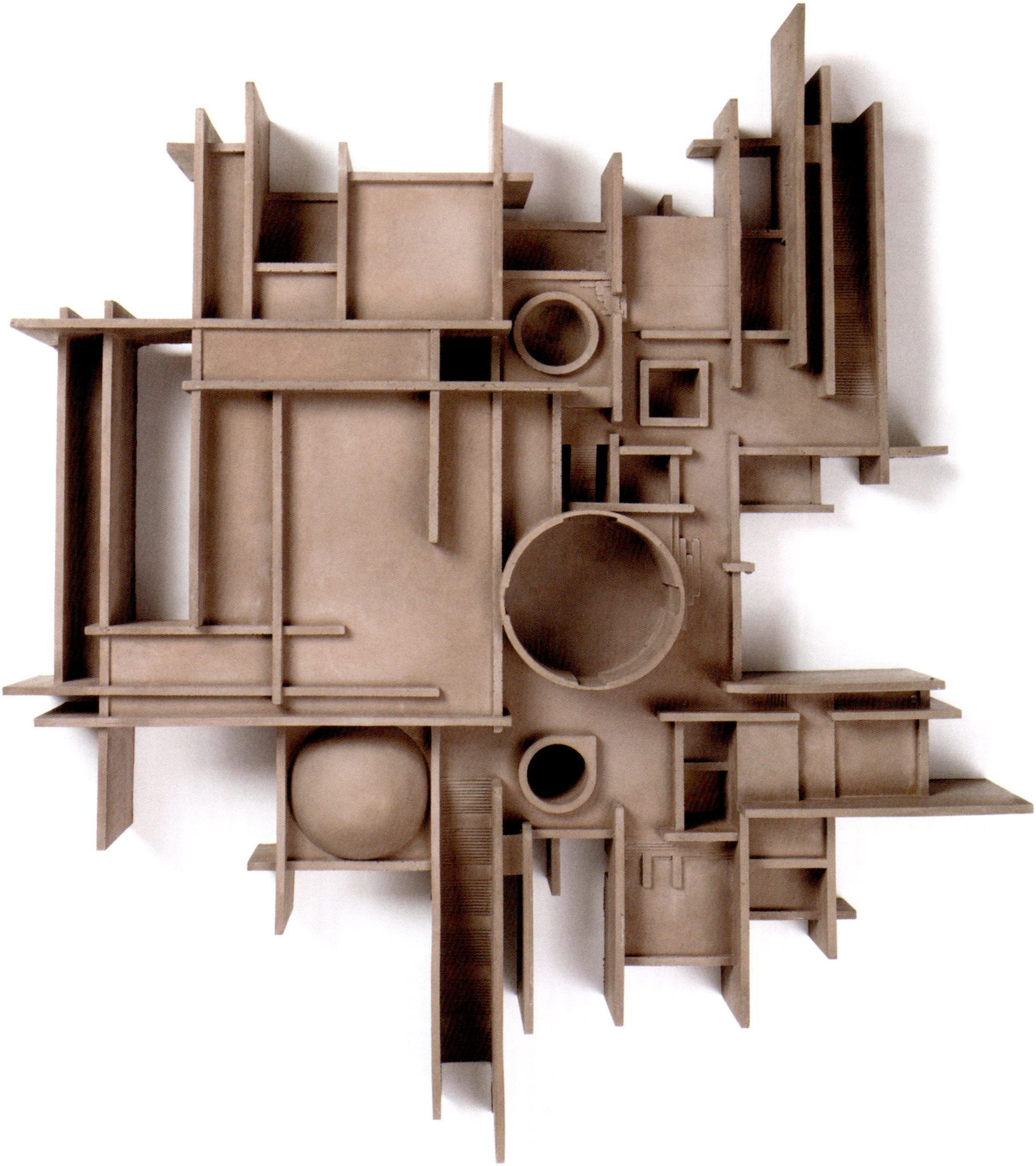

Research Center of the Sea of Cortez pigmented concrete model

Research Center of the Sea of Cortez collages

TATIANA BILBAO ESTUDIO: SELECTED PROJECTS

HOUSING+

ACUÑA HOUSING

In 2015, a series of tornadoes struck the city of Acuña, Coahuila, causing significant devastation, particularly in the neighborhoods of Los Altos de Santa Teresa and Las Aves. This resulted in a tragic aftermath, including injuries, casualties, and the complete destruction of around one hundred homes.

In response to this dire situation, an emergency state was declared in the affected areas, requiring an efficient response to restore the community and improve its original conditions. The INFONAVIT (National Housing Fund Institute) proposed to the community to rebuild the homes using a design strategy that our studio had previously developed for rural and semi-urban areas.

While this design strategy was not originally designed to be implemented as a housing development of standardized homes, it had been conceived with adaptability in different contexts and scenarios in mind, and this proved to be one such context. Consequently, we joined the efforts of the reconstruction, leading to the construction of seventeen houses, and in each one of them adapted the design strategy to the unique needs of each family and its conditions.

The effectiveness of this strategy was evident as it empowered families to make more informed decisions regarding the use of the space compared to the existing homes in the area. At the same time, it helped minimize land usage while maximizing interior space compared to the previous housing model.

Additional to our work in the reconstruction of the houses, we also focused on public space, approaching this project with the aim of creating complementary urban facilities for sports and recreational activities. Despite having limited resources, we prioritized green and shaded areas for social inclusion and to bring a sense of community identity.

Above and Opposite: Housing+ wood model by Taller TORNEL

Housing+ diagram

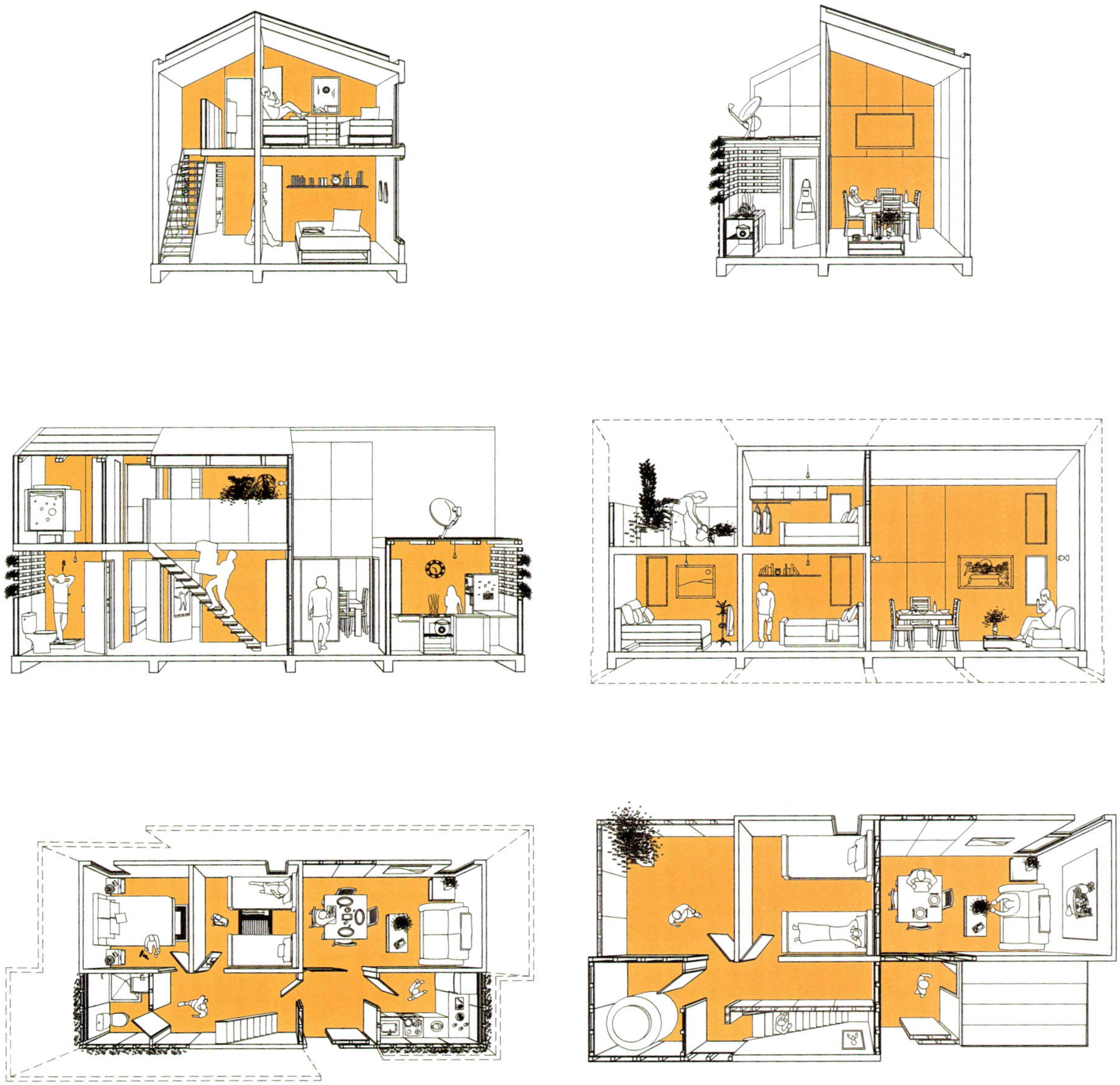

Housing+ section and plan studies

Above and Opposite: Housing+ concept drawings

Above and Opposite: Housing+ concept drawings

Housing+ concept renderings

Housing+ concrete and wood model

Above and opposite: Housing+ prototype

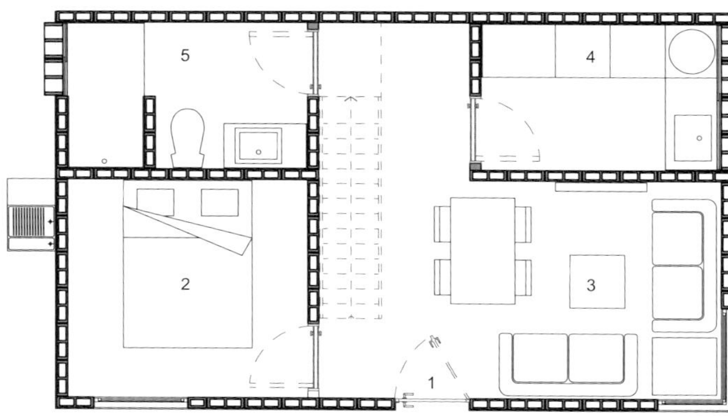

0 m 1 m 2.5 m

SOCIAL HOUSING, ACUÑA
3-ROOMS SINGLE-FAMILY HOME
GROUND FLOOR

1. Entrance
2. First bedroom
3. Dining / Living room
4. Kitchen
5. Bathroom

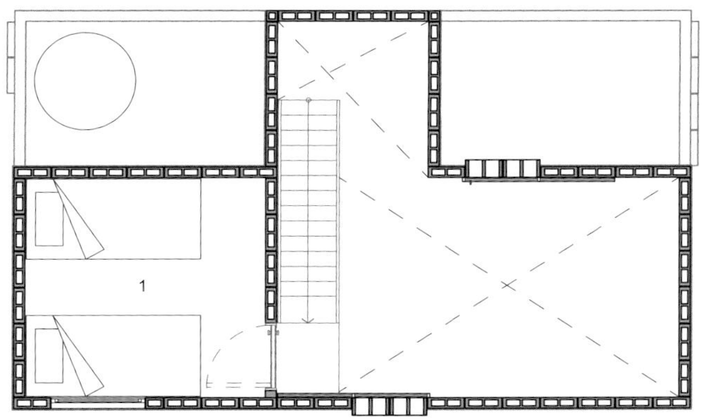

0 m 1 m 2.5 m

SOCIAL HOUSING, ACUÑA
3-ROOMS SINGLE-FAMILY HOME
FIRST FLOOR

1. Second bedroom

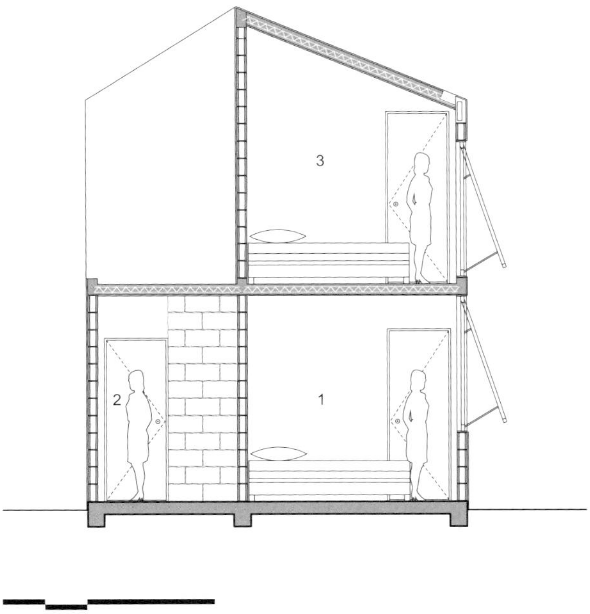

0 m 1 m 2.5 m

SOCIAL HOUSING, ACUÑA
3-ROOMS SINGLE-FAMILY HOME
CROSS CUT

1. First bedroom
2. Bathroom
3. Second bedroom

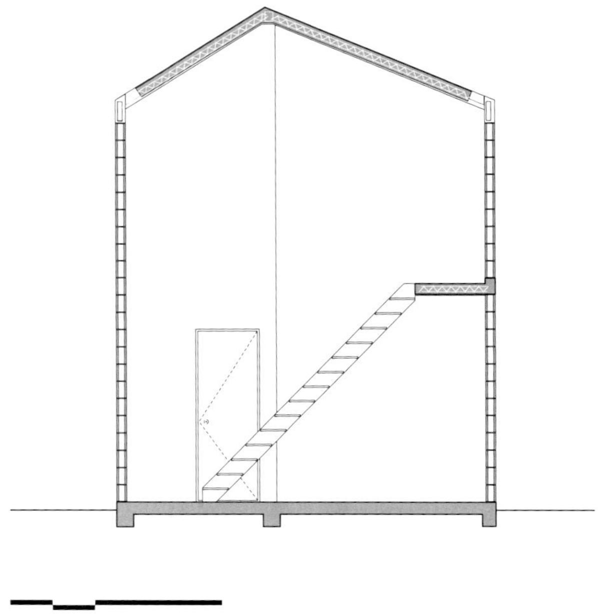

0 m 1 m 2.5 m

SOCIAL HOUSING, ACUÑA
3-ROOMS SINGLE-FAMILY HOME
CROSS CUT

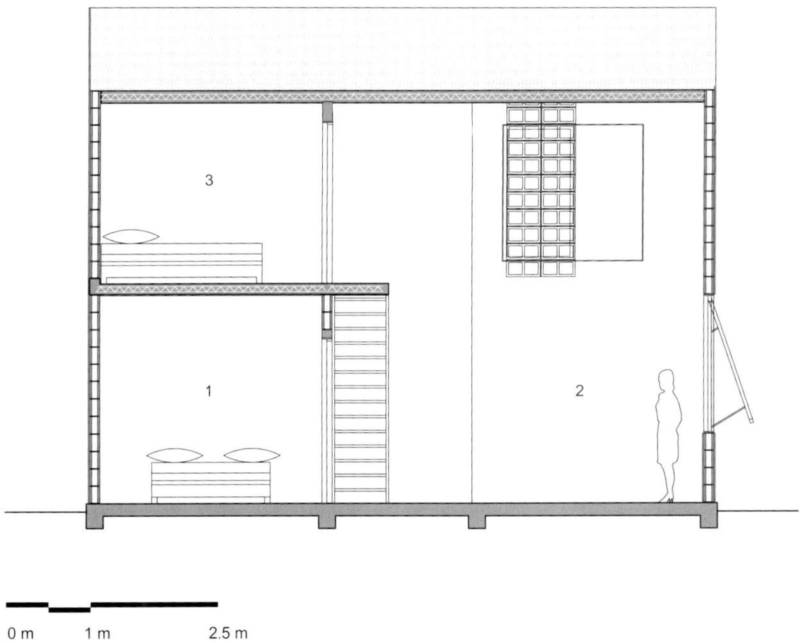

SOCIAL HOUSING, ACUÑA
3-ROOMS SINGLE-FAMILY HOME
LONGITUDINAL CUT

1. First bedroom
2. Dining / Living room
3. Second bedroom

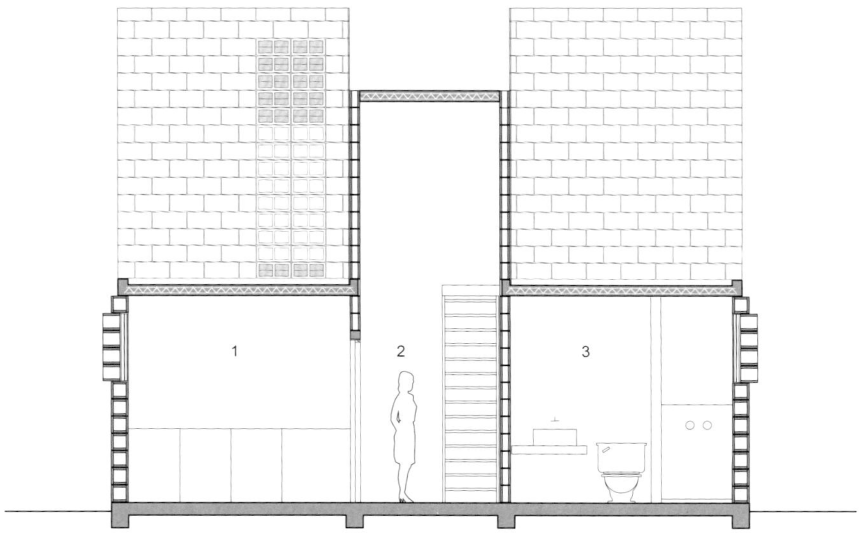

0 m 1 m 2.5 m

SOCIAL HOUSING, ACUÑA
3-ROOMS SINGLE-FAMILY HOME
LONGITUDINAL CUT

1. Kitchen
2. Hallway
3. Bathroom

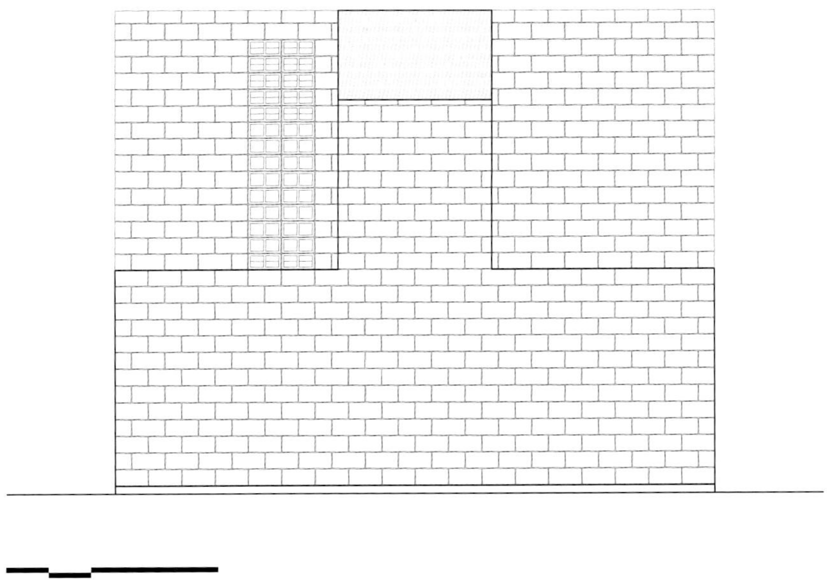

0 m 1 m 2.5 m

SOCIAL HOUSING, ACUÑA
3-ROOMS SINGLE-FAMILY HOME
FACADE

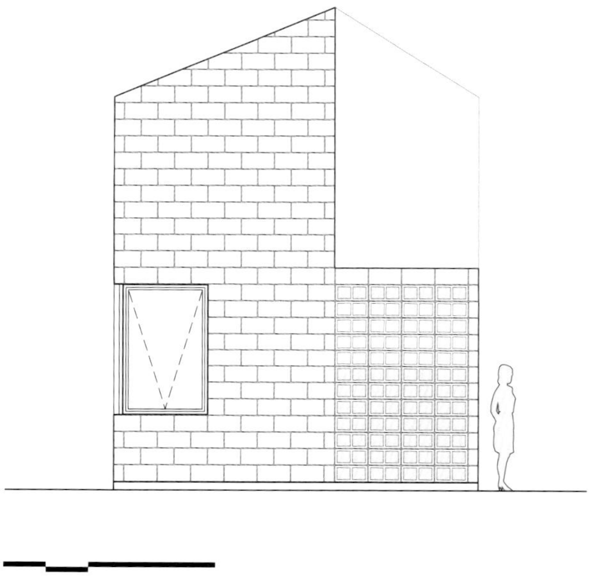

0 m 1 m 2.5 m

SOCIAL HOUSING, ACUÑA
3-ROOMS SINGLE-FAMILY HOME
FACADE

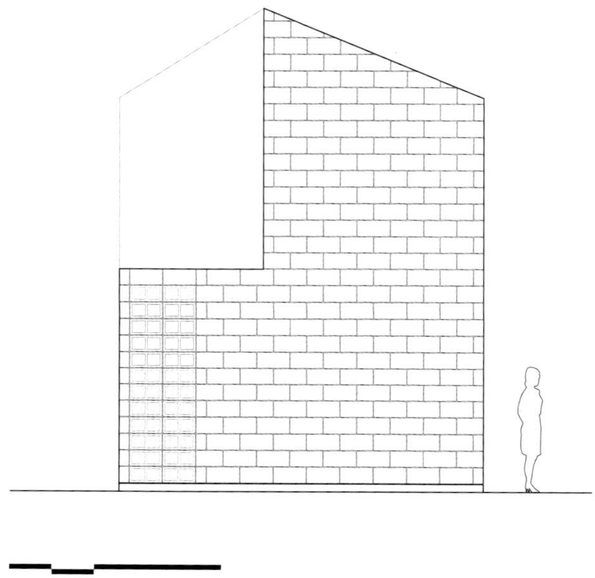

0 m 1 m 2.5 m

SOCIAL HOUSING, ACUÑA
3-ROOMS SINGLE-FAMILY HOME
FACADE

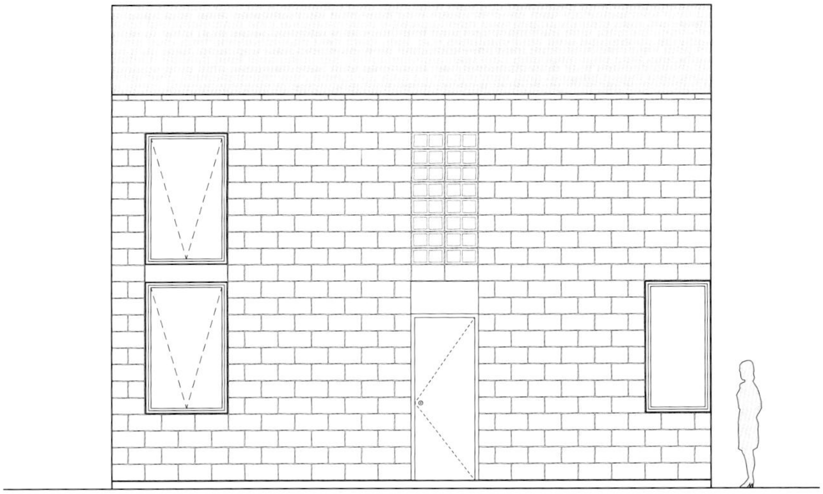

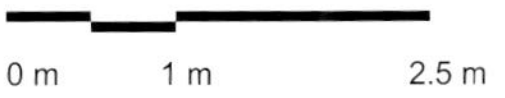

SOCIAL HOUSING, ACUÑA
3-ROOMS SINGLE-FAMILY HOME
FACADE

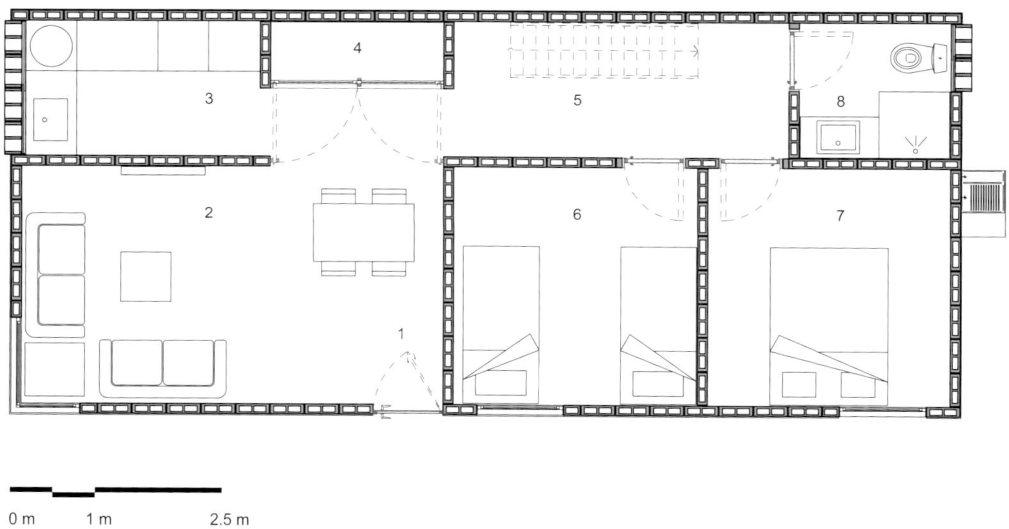

SOCIAL HOUSING, ACUÑA
4-ROOMS SINGLE-FAMILY HOME
GROUND FLOOR

1. Entrance
2. Dining / Living room
3. Kitchen
4. Storage
5. Hallway
6. First bedroom
7. Second bedroom
8. Bathroom

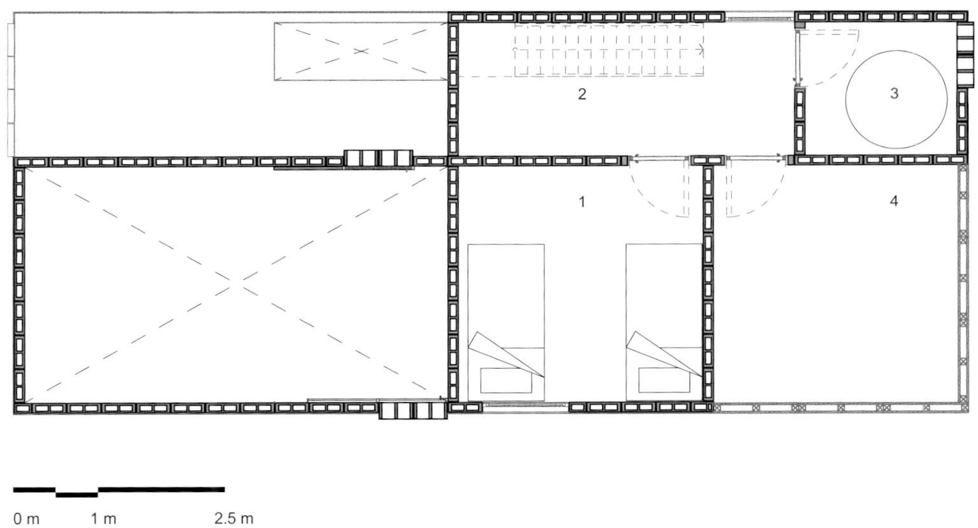

SOCIAL HOUSING, ACUÑA
4-ROOMS SINGLE-FAMILY HOME
FIRST FLOOR

1. Third bedroom
2. Hallway
3. Water storage tank
4. Terrace

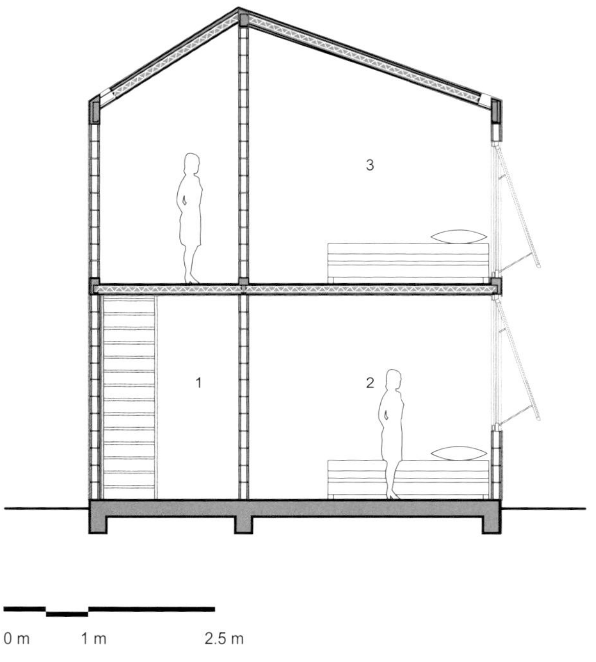

SOCIAL HOUSING, ACUÑA
4-ROOMS SINGLE-FAMILY HOME
CROSS CUT

1. Hallway
2. First bedroom
3. Third bedroom

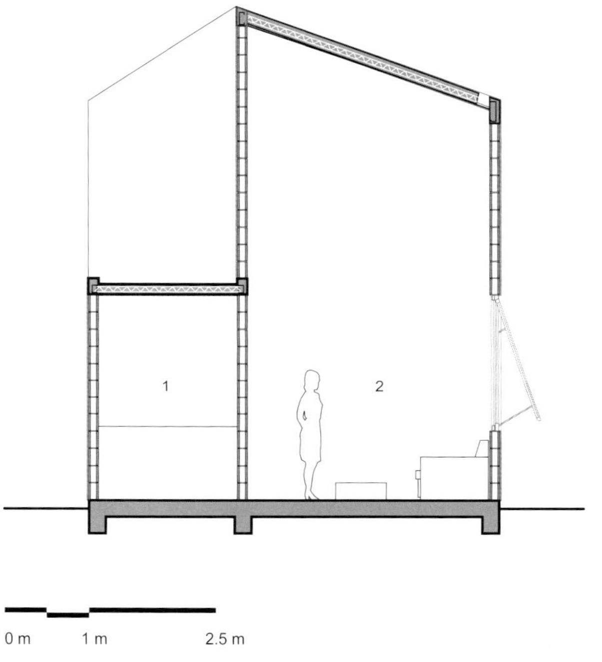

SOCIAL HOUSING, ACUÑA
4-ROOMS SINGLE-FAMILY HOME
CROSS CUT

1. Kitchen
2. Dining / Living room

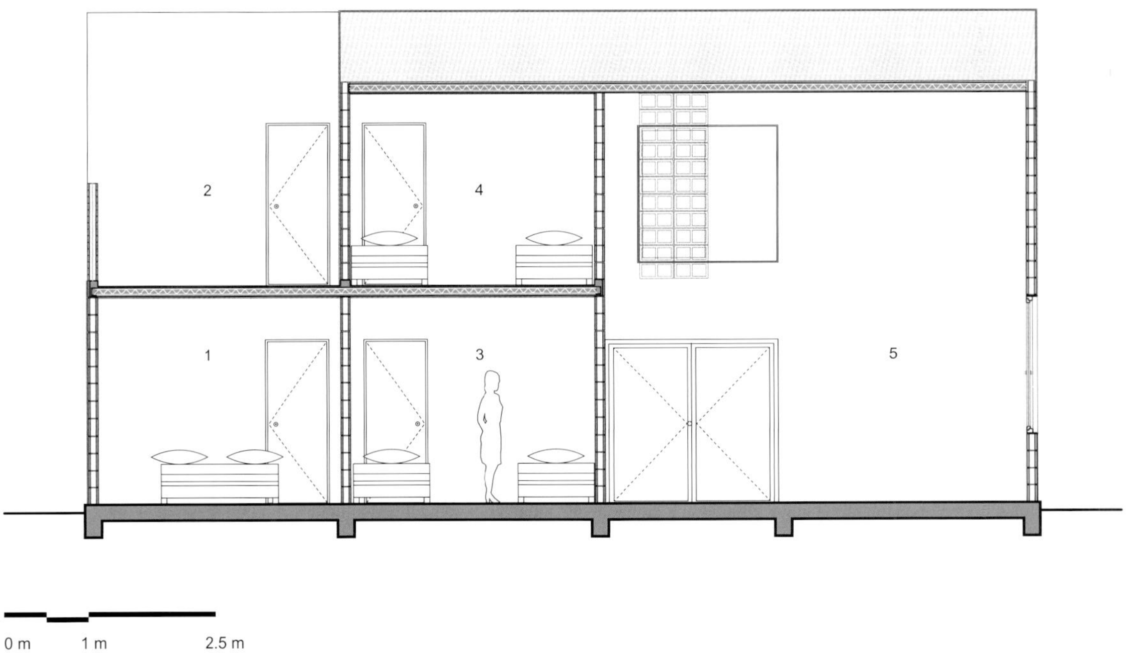

SOCIAL HOUSING, ACUÑA
4-ROOMS SINGLE-FAMILY HOME
LONGITUDINAL CUT

1. Second bedroom
2. Terrace
3. First bedroom
4. Third bedroom
5. Entrance / Living room

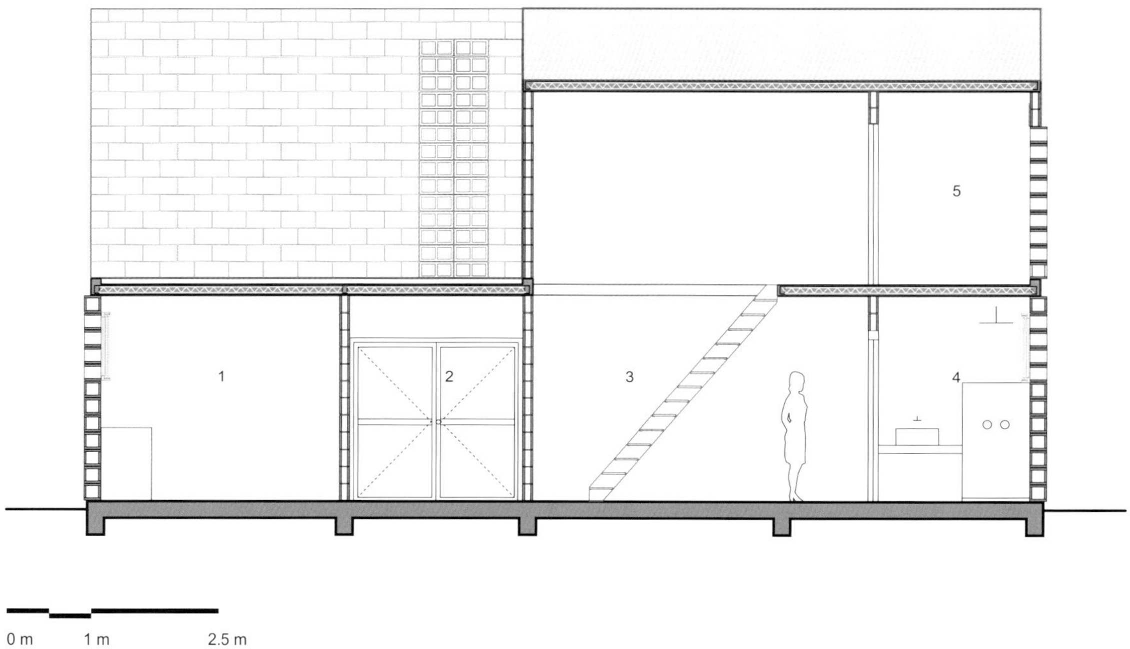

SOCIAL HOUSING, ACUÑA
4-ROOMS SINGLE-FAMILY HOME
LONGITUDINAL CUT

1. Kitchen
2. Storage
3. Hallway
4. Bathroom
5. Water storage tank

0 m 1 m 2.5 m

SOCIAL HOUSING, ACUÑA
4-ROOMS SINGLE-FAMILY HOME
FACADE

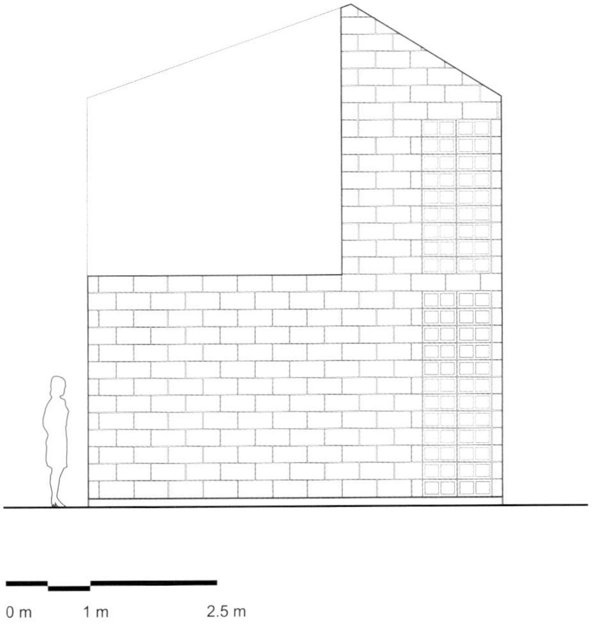

SOCIAL HOUSING, ACUÑA
4-ROOMS SINGLE-FAMILY HOME
FACADE

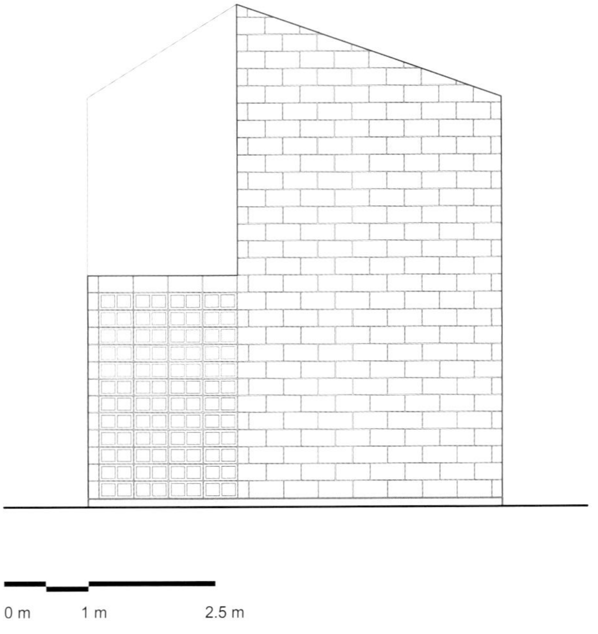

SOCIAL HOUSING, ACUÑA
4-ROOMS SINGLE-FAMILY HOME
FACADE

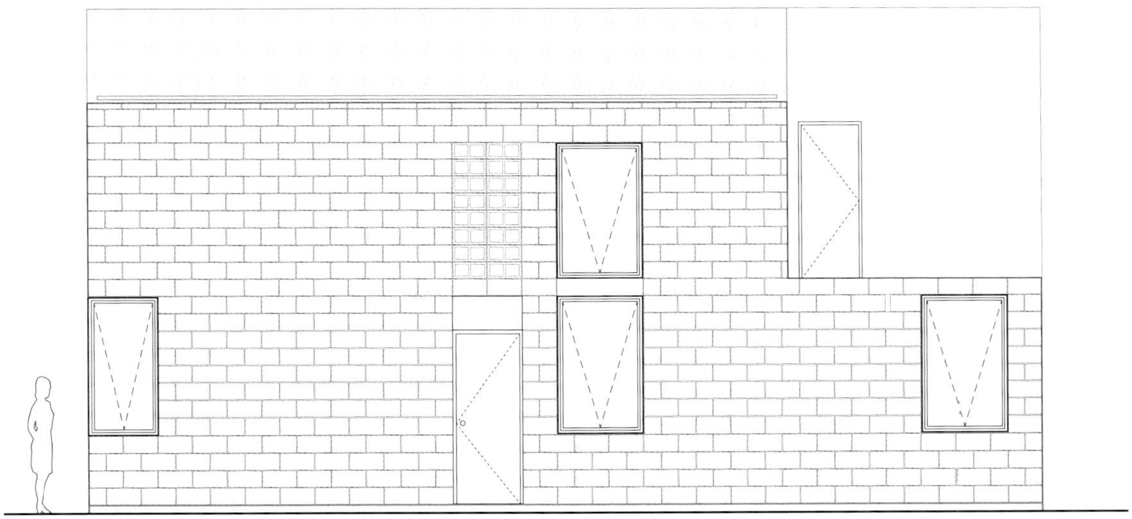

0 m 1 m 2.5 m

SOCIAL HOUSING, ACUÑA
4-ROOMS SINGLE-FAMILY HOME
FACADE

ACUÑA PUBLIC SPACE

In addition to our efforts in reconstructing the houses destroyed during the 2015 tornado outbreak in the city of Acuña, we also focused in enhancing the public spaces of the community. We approached the task of enriching the existing urban life by providing residents with sports and recreational facilities. Despite facing a limiting budget, we prioritized the design and construction of communal spaces, emphasizing shade and greenery. We strategically crafted connections and pathways throughout the complex to enhance safety and mobility for residents.

Our project for the renovation of the public space has profoundly transformed the social dynamics of the neighborhood, incorporating key elements into the urban fabric: three parks, a pedestrian walkway, and a memorial dedicated to the tornado victims. Each of these elements has been designed to have aesthetic unity and visual coherence, even when they are not physically contiguous. Their design and materiality result in engaging changes in pavements, cladding, and vegetation, creating an immersive experience that connects people with their environment.

Acuña Public Space

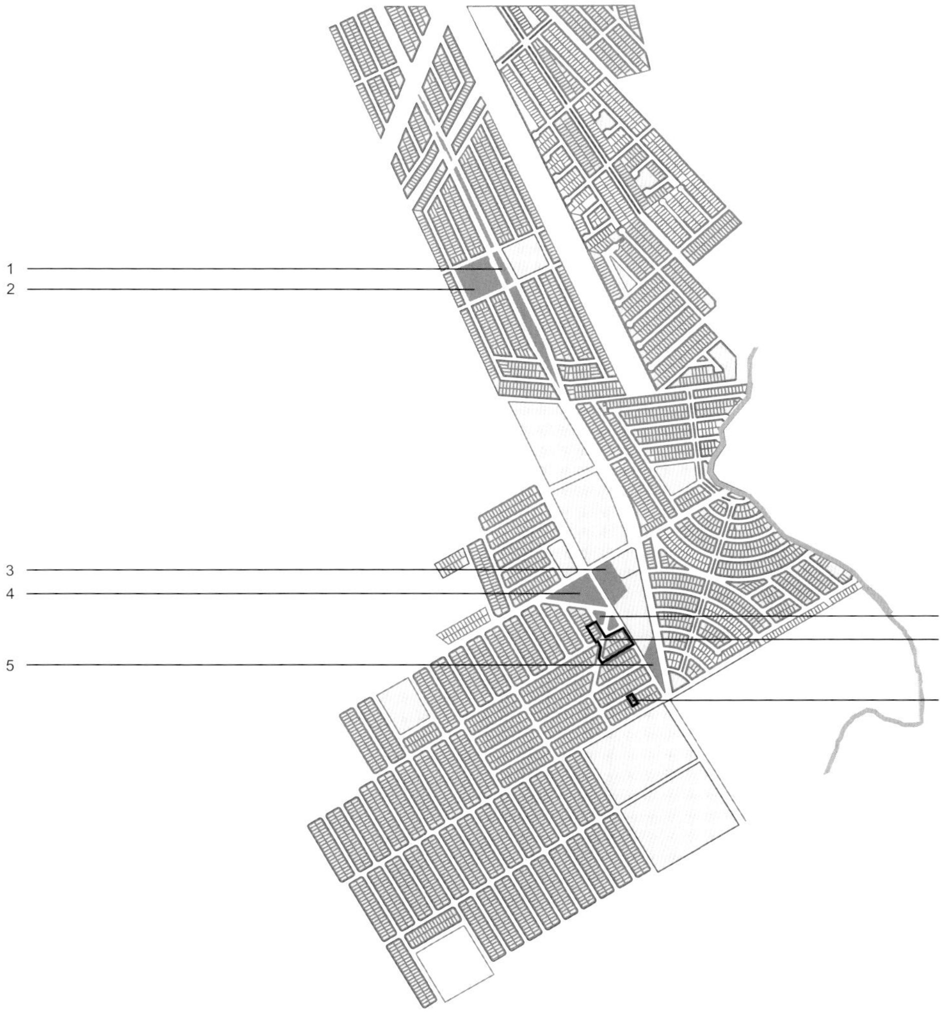

SOCIAL HOUSING, ACUÑA
PUBLIC SPACES PLAN

1. Parque Lineal
2. Plaza Central
3. Sport Zone
4. CDC
5. Memorial
6. Glorietas
7. Social Housing project from Tatiana Bilbao ESTUDIO

SOCIAL HOUSING, ACUÑA
PUBLIC SPACES
PARQUE LINEAL

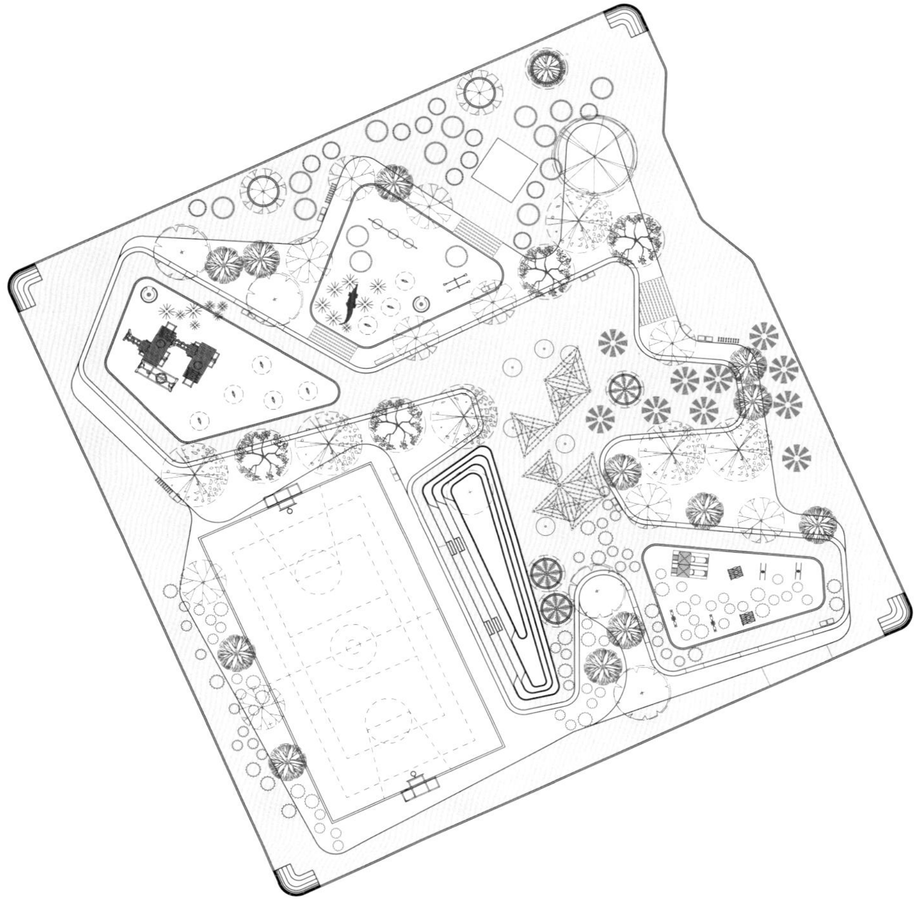

SOCIAL HOUSING, ACUÑA
PUBLIC SPACES
PLAZA CENTRAL

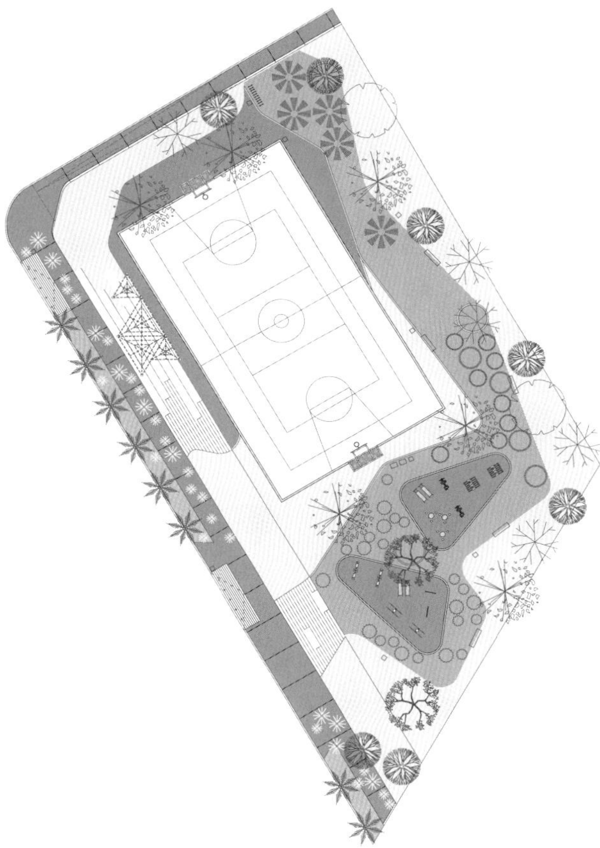

0 m 5 m 10 m 20 m

SOCIAL HOUSING, ACUÑA
PUBLIC SPACES
SPORT ZONE

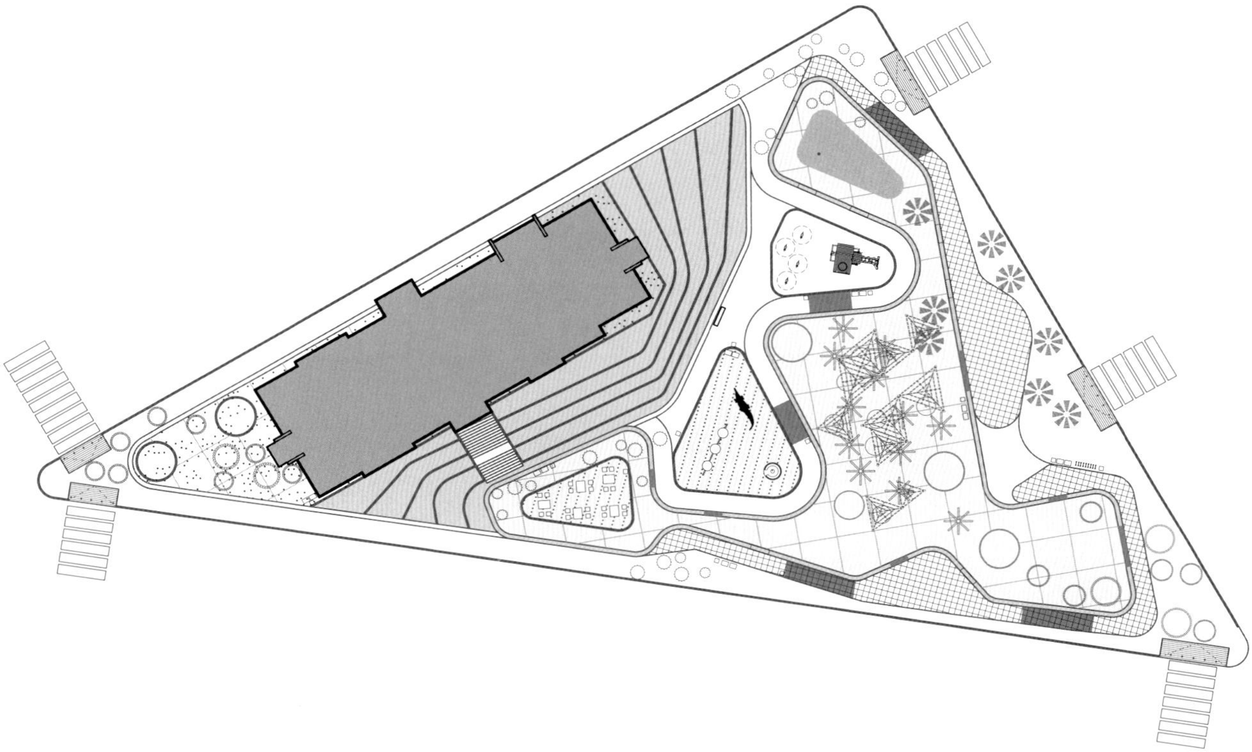

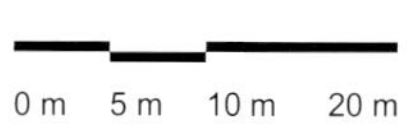

SOCIAL HOUSING, ACUÑA
PUBLIC SPACES
CDC

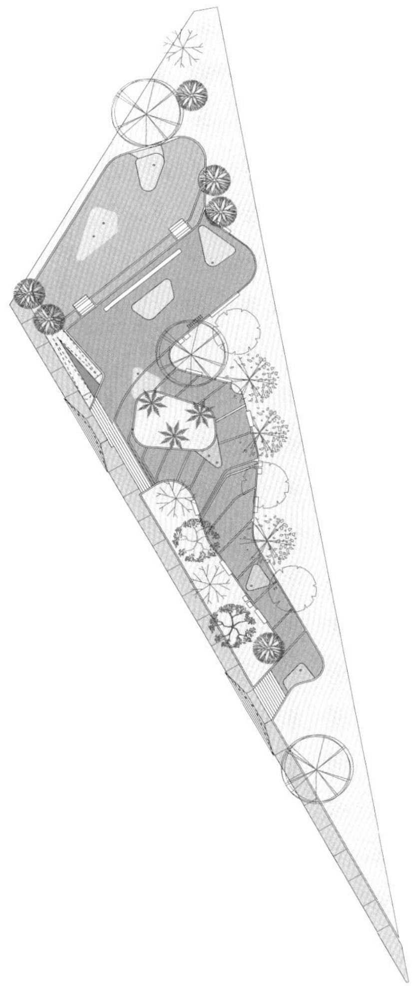

0 m 10 m 25 m 50 m

SOCIAL HOUSING, ACUÑA
PUBLIC SPACES
MEMORIAL

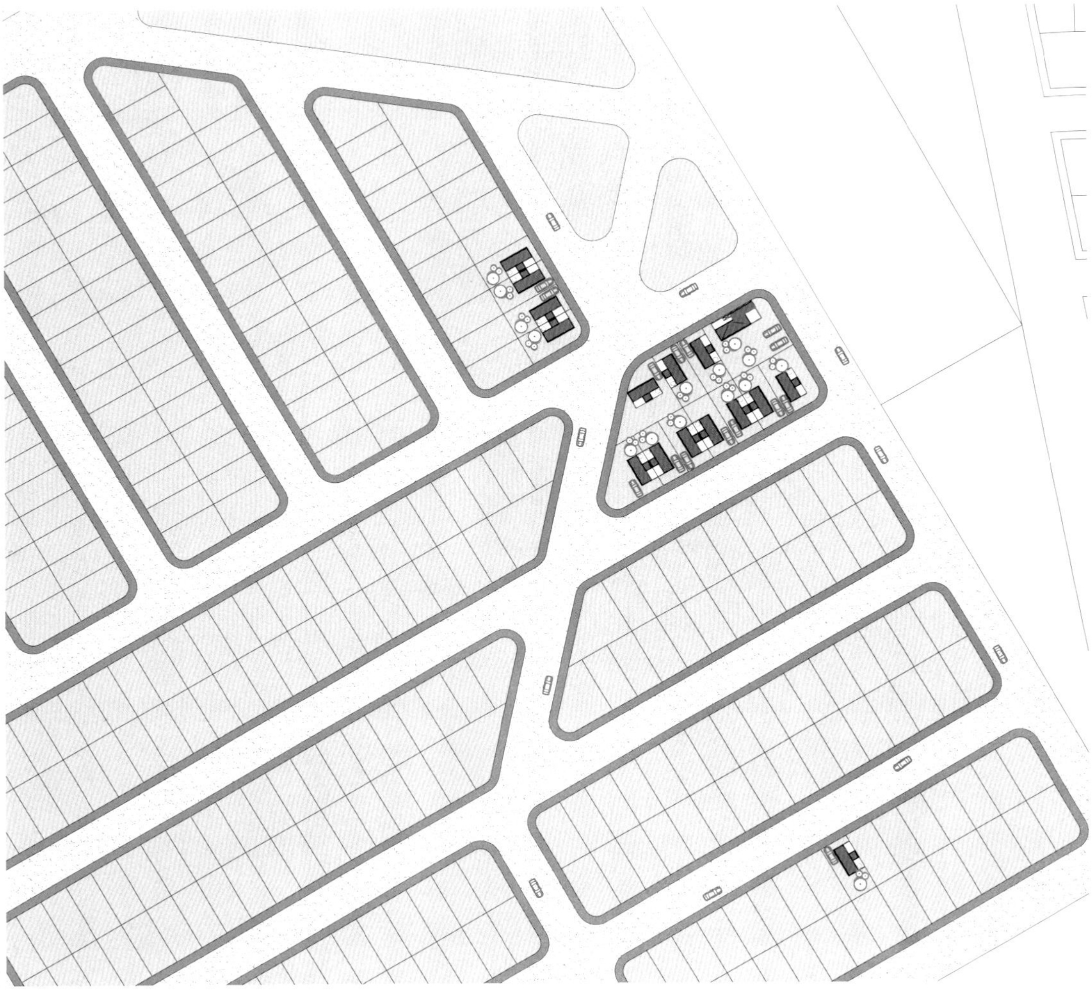

0 m 10 m 25 m 50 m

SOCIAL HOUSING, ACUÑA
PUBLIC SPACES
GLORIETAS

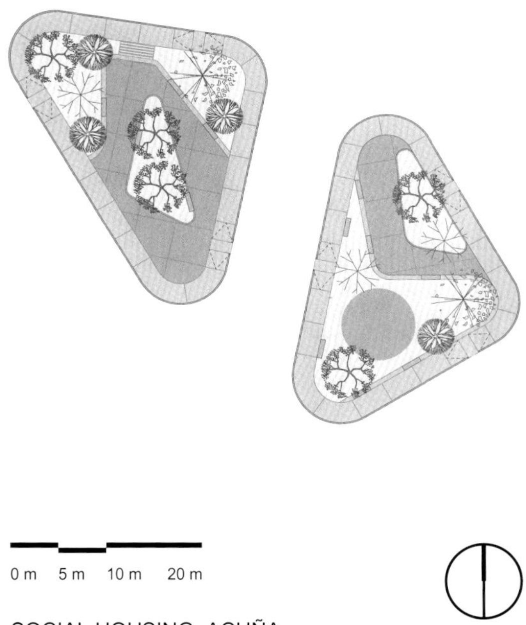

SOCIAL HOUSING, ACUÑA
PUBLIC SPACES
GLORIETAS

LYON LA CONFLUENCE, Ilot A3

In 2007, the city of Lyon embarked on the revitalization of La Confluence, a former industrial district. Herzog & de Meuron were commissioned to develop the master plan for the second phase of the project, with the additional task of designing the inaugural block (*ilot* in French) to mark the beginning of this new extension. Under the idea of "unity within diversity," a group of international architects were invited to work in the development of each of the buildings (*bâtiments*).

We were invited to design three buildings: two for social housing (Bâtiment 3 and Bâtiment 7) and one for private housing (Bâtiment 8). Since the beginning, it was clear to us the importance of creating not only stacked living units, but also to imagine an inclusive space that could promote encounters and relationships among members of the community, encouraging people to use the city as an extension of their domestic space.

The buildings encompass and face a common semi-public courtyard with open access to everyone in the heart of the block. In all three buildings, we made use of vertical circulation, terraces, and open areas to promote encounter and allow the possibility for all types of relationships to happen.

Bâtiment 3 is a social housing building designed to allow a broad range of different spatial configurations, using double-height and *demi-niveau*, all of the twenty-one units are in contact with the exterior in a different way. We created a complex central-core concrete volume carved by double-height terraces, corner balconies, and consistent windows trough the facade. These elements, defined by its yellow pine wood materiality, make evident the relationship between the interior and the neighborhood.

Bâtiment 7 is the second social housing building of the project and faces the main public plaza on one side and the interior courtyard on the other. We designed a volume that houses twenty-one units, distributing them around a centrally exposed staircase that overlooks the courtyard. Here, too, each unit is different in size and distribution, resulting in a dynamic facade with balconies and terraces facing the plaza. In these two buildings, the strategy of defining each unit as unique was aimed at allowing its inhabitants to understand that their differences bring the community together.

Bâtiment 8 sits west of Bâtiment 7, and is the only one designated for market-rate housing. In this case, we explored the notion of a homogeneous set of twenty-three units forming a single volume facing the main plaza. This simple gesture invites its inhabitants to become conscious that together they form part of one community.

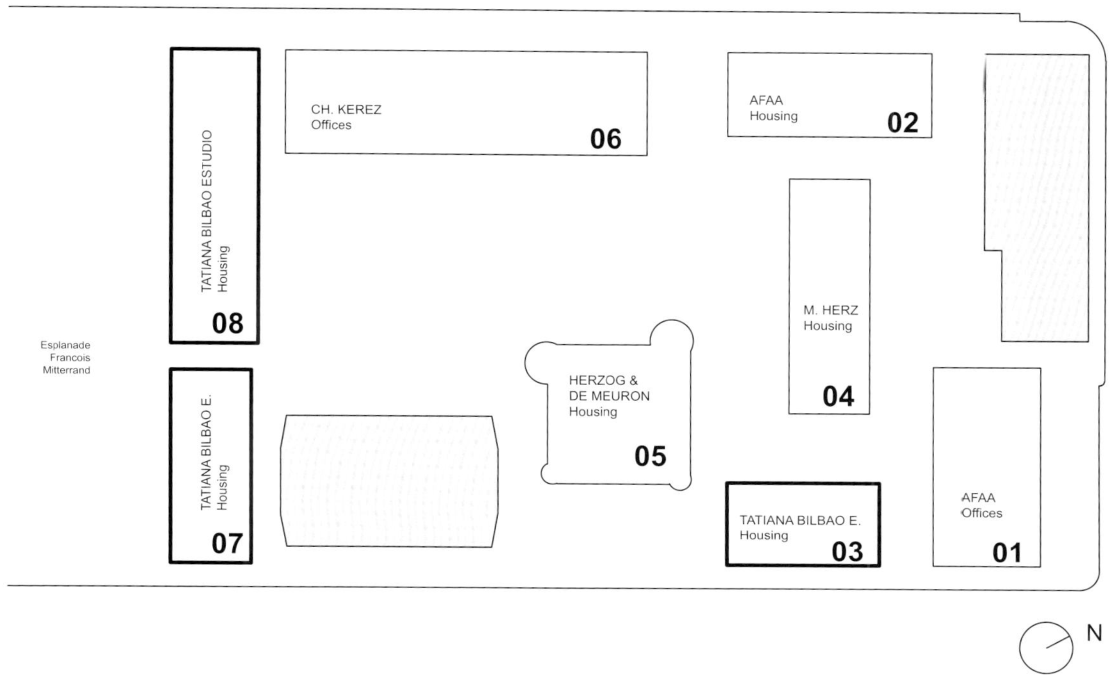

Lyon La Confluence models

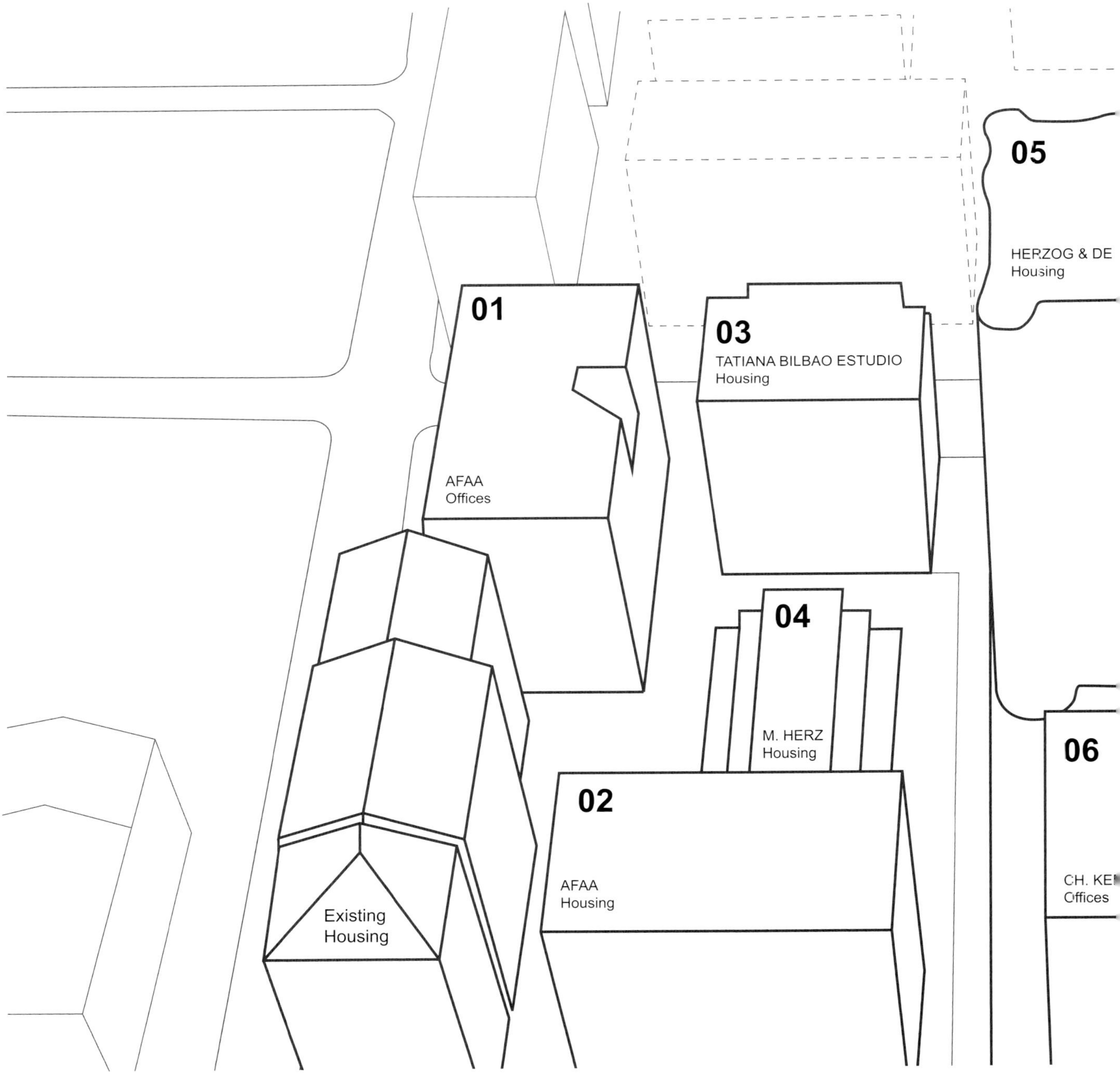
05
HERZOG & DE
Housing
01
AFAA
Offices
03
TATIANA BILBAO ESTUDIO
Housing
04
M. HERZ
Housing
06
02
AFAA
Housing
CH. KE
Offices
Existing
Housing

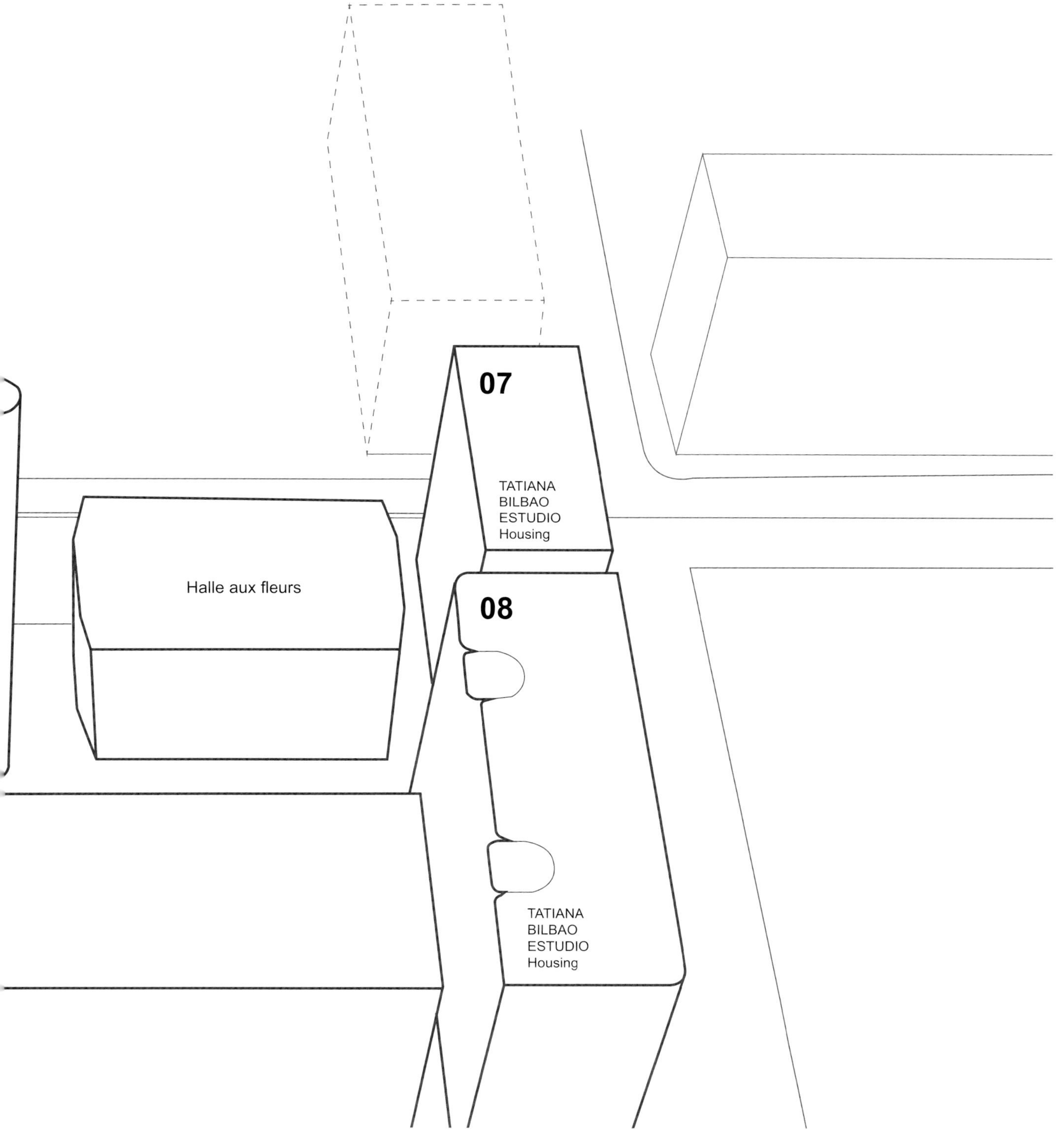
07
TATIANA
BILBAO
ESTUDIO
Housing
Halle aux fleurs
08
TATIANA
BILBAO
ESTUDIO
Housing

Bâtiment 3

Bâtiment 8

Bâtiment 7

Above: Bâtiment 7 & 8 from plaza; Below: Bâtiment 8

LYON CONFLUENCE
B3 - FLOOR

1. Living Room
2. Kitchen
3. Bedroom
4. Bathroom
5. Corridor
6. Terrace
7. Stairs

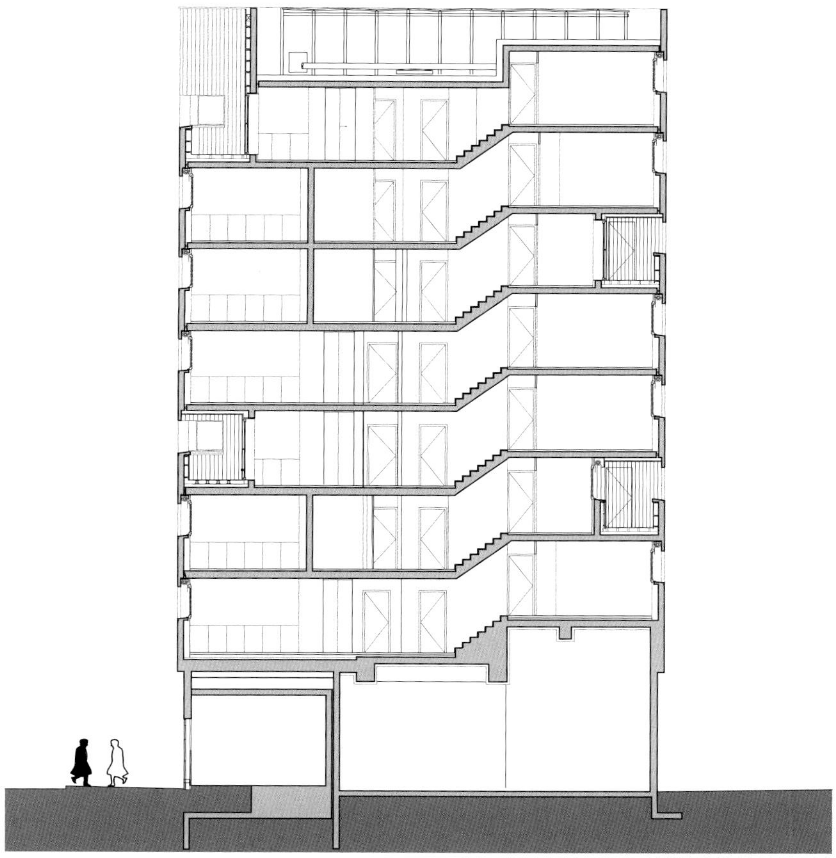

LYON CONFLUENCE
B3 - SECTION

LYON CONFLUENCE
B3 - FACADE

Above: Bâtiment 3 porch; Below: Bâtiment 3 from plaza

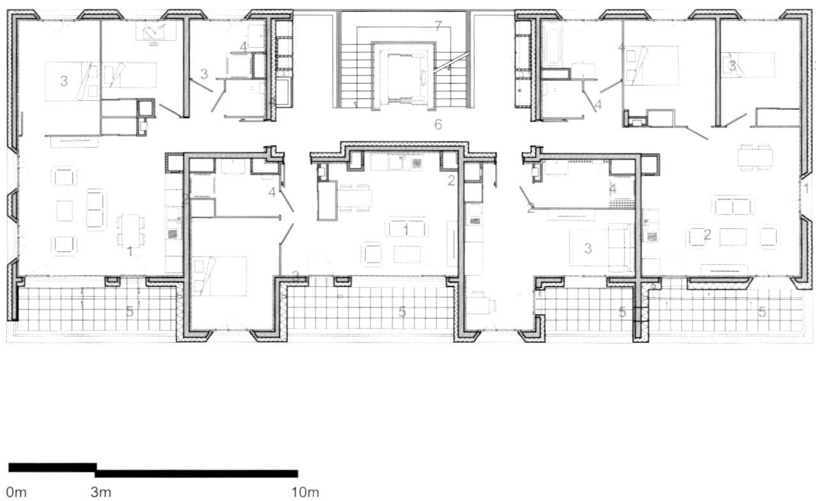

LYON CONFLUENCE
B7 - FLOOR

1. Living Room
2. Kitchen
3. Bedroom
4. Bathroom
5. Corridor
6. Terrace
7. Stairs

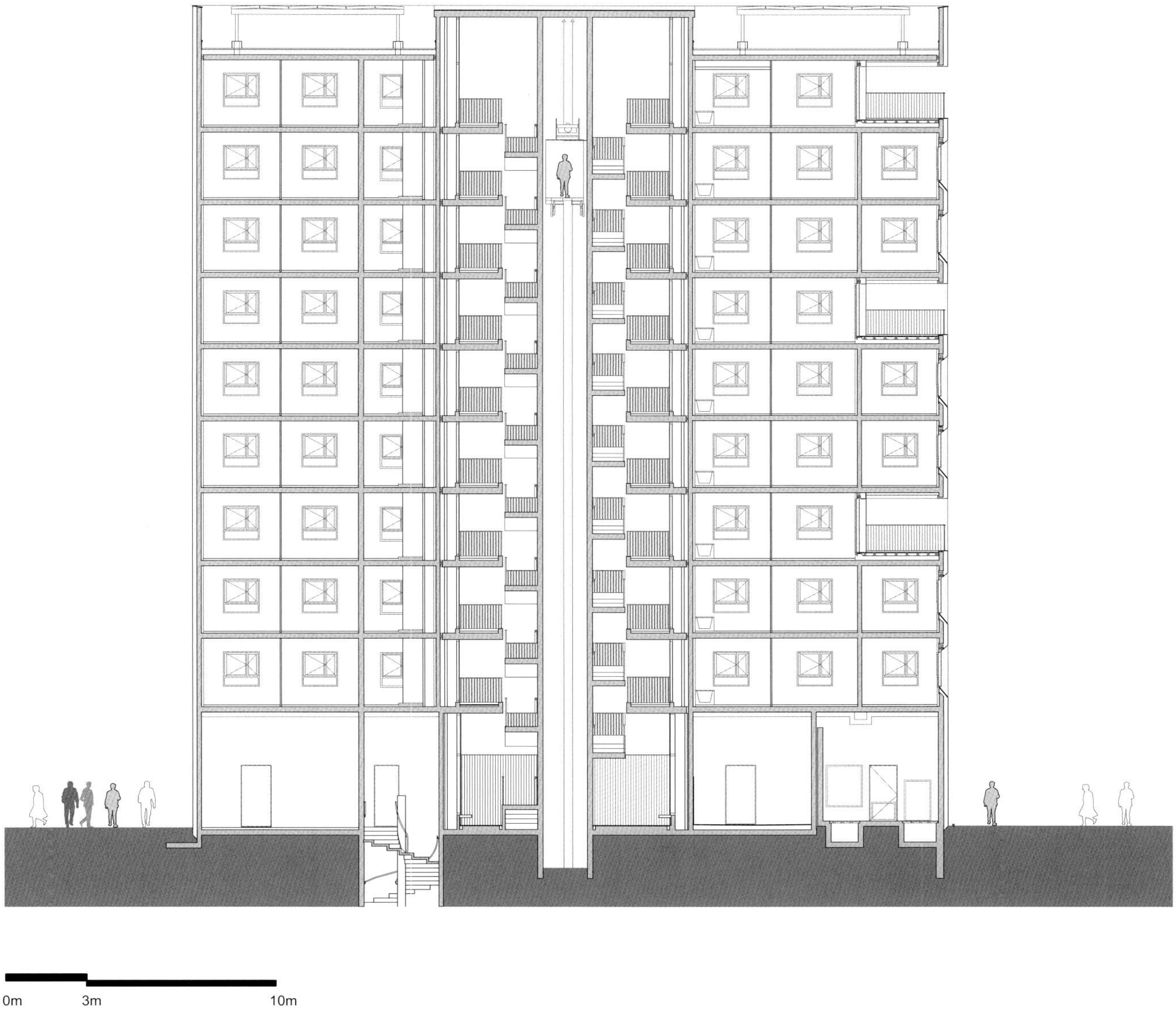

LYON CONFLUENCE
B7 - SECTION

LYON CONFLUENCE
B7 - FACADE

Above: Bâtiment 7 porch; Below: Bâtiment 7

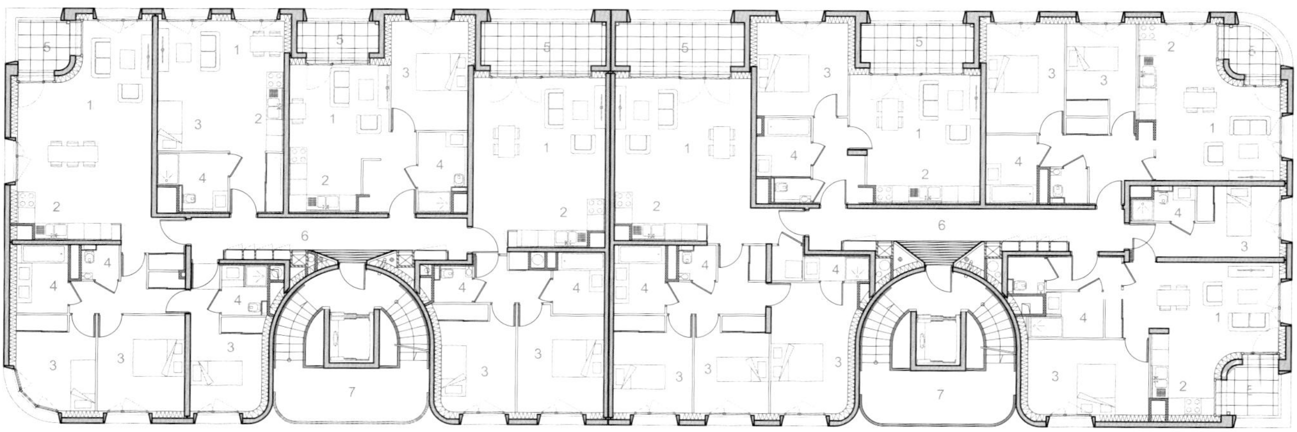

0m 3m 10m

LYON CONFLUENCE
B8 - FLOOR

1. Living Room
2. Kitchen
3. Bedroom
4. Bathroom
5. Corridor
6. Terrace
7. Stairs

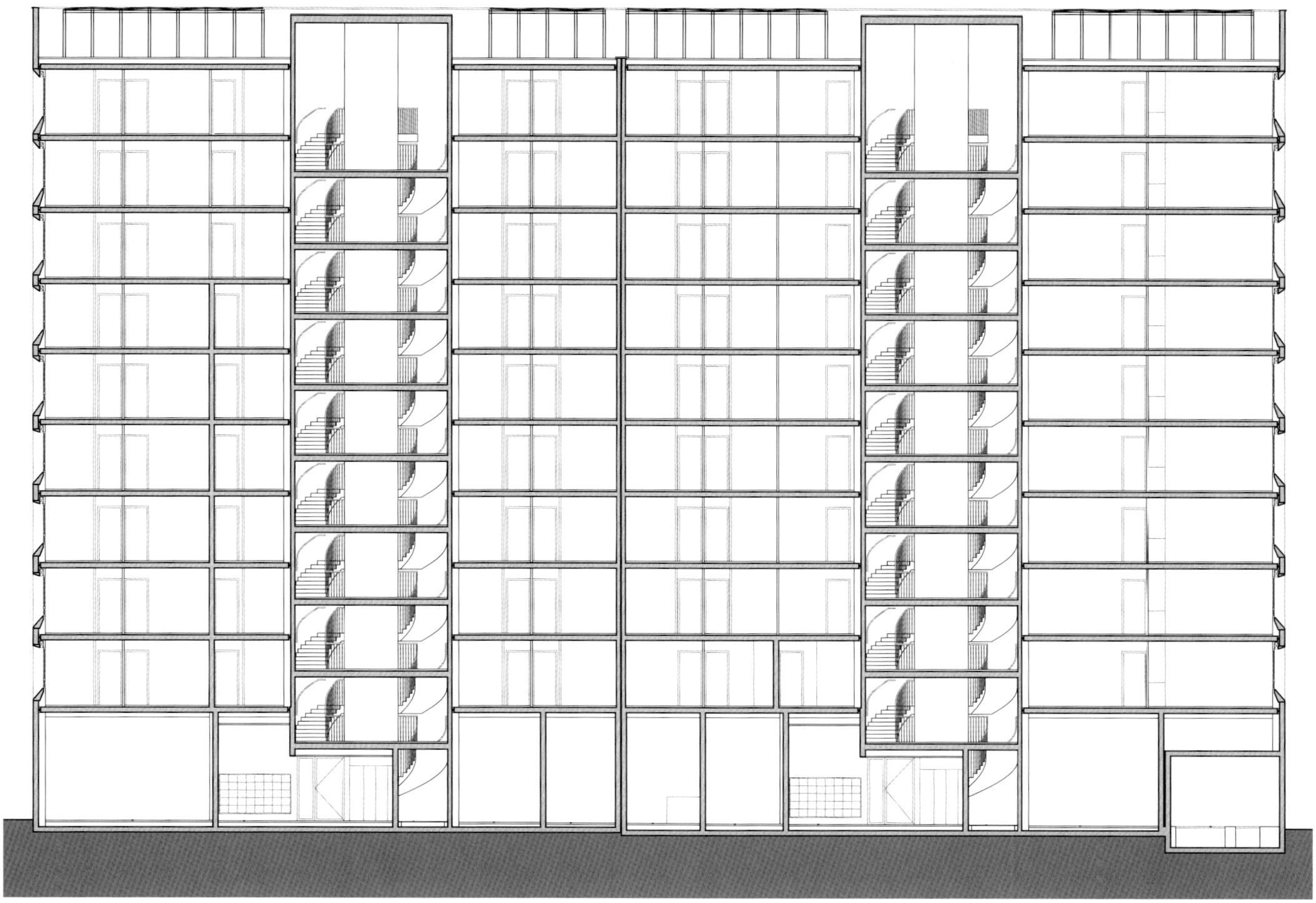

0m 3m 10m

LYON CONFLUENCE
B8 - SECTION

LYON CONFLUENCE
B8 - FACADE

Bâtiment 8 porch

Lyon La Confluence view nto courtyarc

Lyon La Confluence view into courtyard

Lyon La Confluence view into courtyard

Lyon La Conf uence view between buildings

OLIVE WEST

Olive West is a densification project adjacent to downtown St. Louis, consisting of a neighborhood plan of town and garden houses. With a collaborative approach in mind, we invited a team of renowned architects to work on the design of the houses, including MOS Architects (USA), Productora (Mexico-USA), and Estudio Macías Peredo (Mexico).

Emily Rauh Pulitzer, philanthropist and founder of the Pulitzer Arts Foundation, initiated this project as an attempt to understand the housing typology of this century. Neglected for decades due to its typical single-row, townhouse typology, this neighborhood has been suffocating since St. Louis' major economic crisis in the 70s. However, situated among a confluence of residential, commercial, educational, and cultural spaces, it has attracted a booming interest of revival. Named after the street that it revolves around, Olive West recognizes the need for quality housing that predisposes communal development through shared spaces, and aims for more inclusive ways of living.

The neighborhood plan provides a gradient of activity along its length, beginning with the meeting places in and around the rehabilitated historic Wolfner Building, and extending eastward to increasingly scattered spaces for communal enjoyment and social gatherings. These spaces are situated between the houses and help blur the boundary between private lots, turning the project into a continuous landscape. The resulting symbiosis of private and communal outdoor spaces is what creates the project's park-like atmosphere. Layers of varied privacy and publicness make these outdoor spaces comfortable for different kinds of activity.

Historic architectural elements, statues, and large-scale objects were recovered from the National Buildings Arts Center and placed in the shared gardens. In their new context, they become curious objects of uncertain use, and their presence invites incidental interaction, creating an open gallery where each artifact tells the story of the site through its past life.

Above and Opposite: Olive West concept collages

Above and Opposite: Olive West concept collages

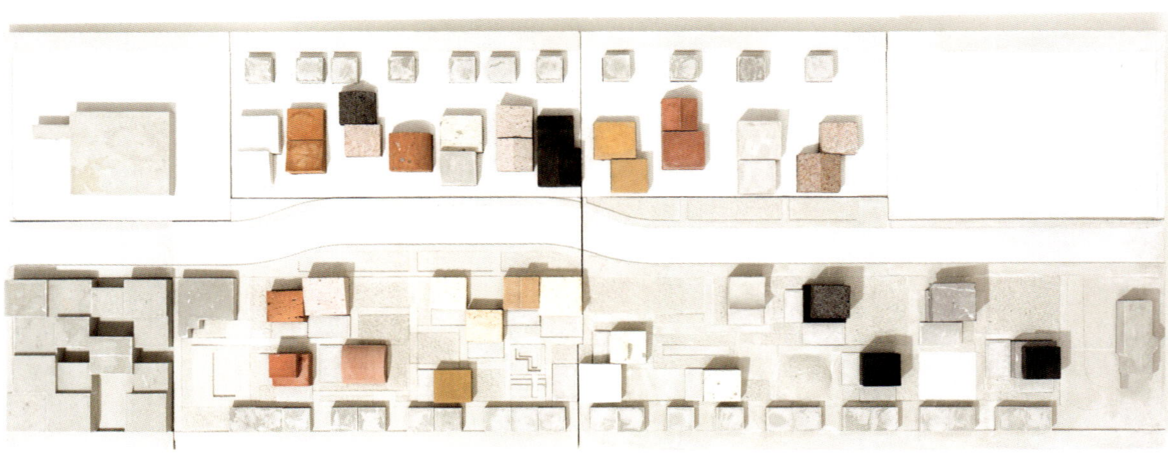

Above and Opposite: Olive West pigmented concrete concept models

Olive West pigmented concrete concept models

Above: Olive West Site Plan; Below: Olive West

Dielmann
Sotheby's

OLIVE WEST SOUTH

Our design of Olive West South, a garden house inspired by the traditional dog-trot house, includes a central breezeway to ventilate the adjacent rooms during the hot and humid summers. The massing of the house is perpendicularly stacked to provide shade to the ground-floor porches while creating two modest roof gardens above, doubling the amount of potential usable outdoor living space for the family and creating various possibilities for private and public activities.

Concept
2 Bars, 2 'Public Rooms", 2 Views

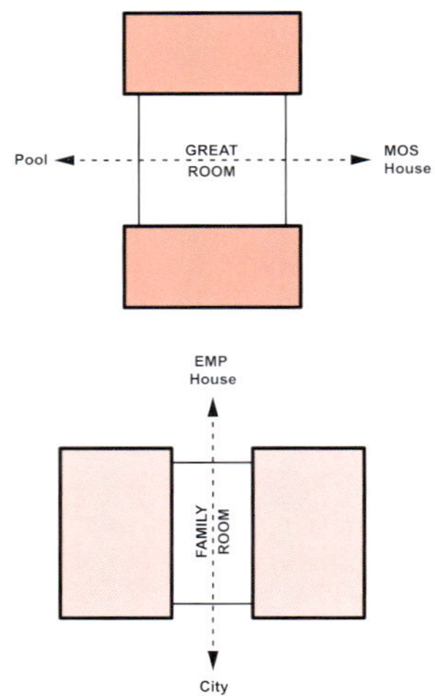

Concept
Superimposition of bars

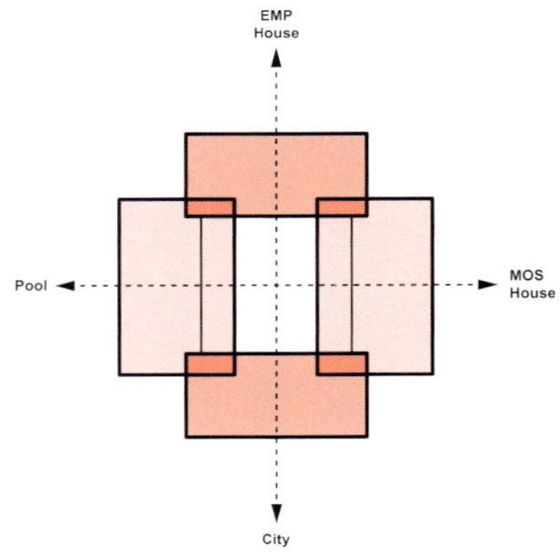

Olive West South concept collage

Olive West South concept sketches

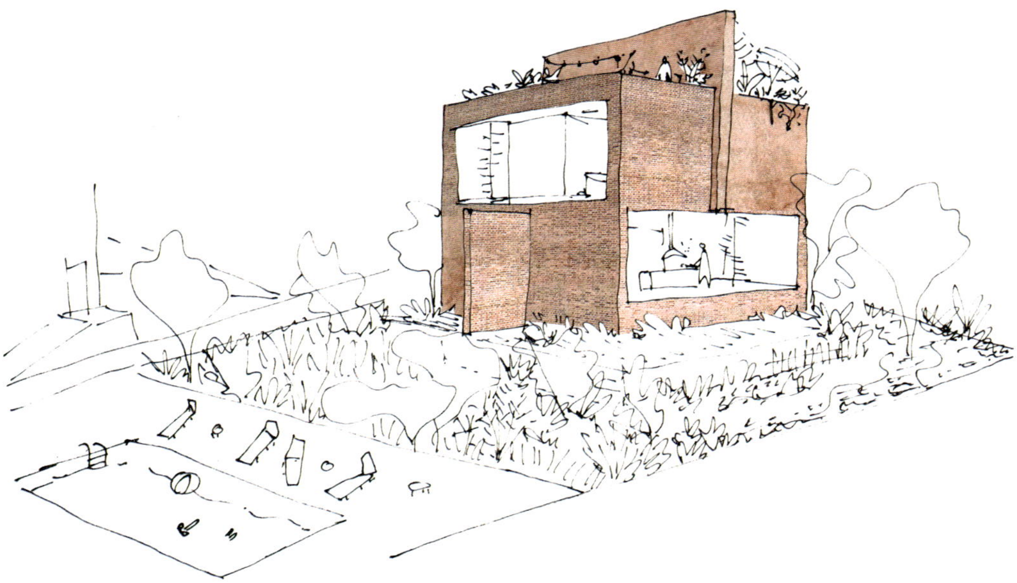

Above and Opposite: Olive West South concept sketches

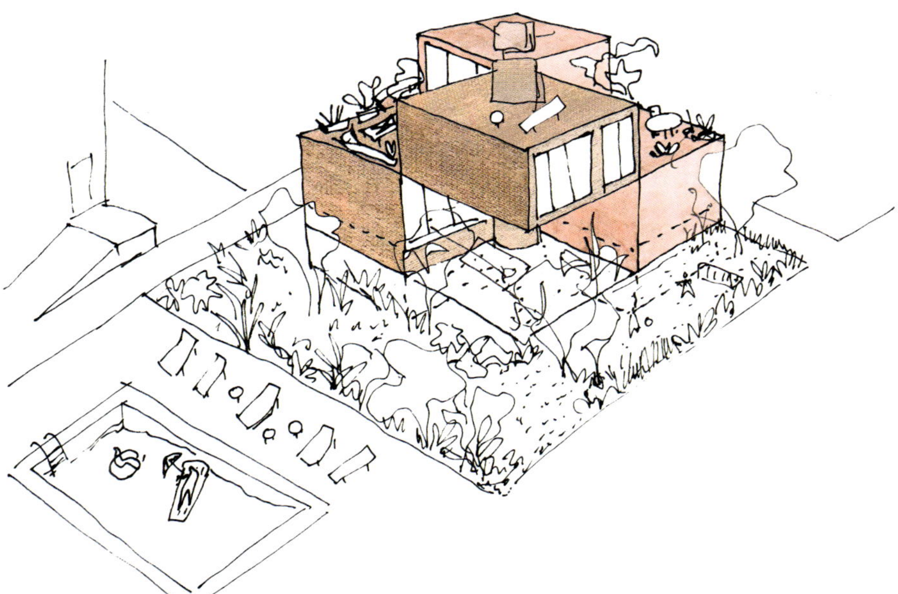

Above and Opposite: Olive West South pigmented concrete model

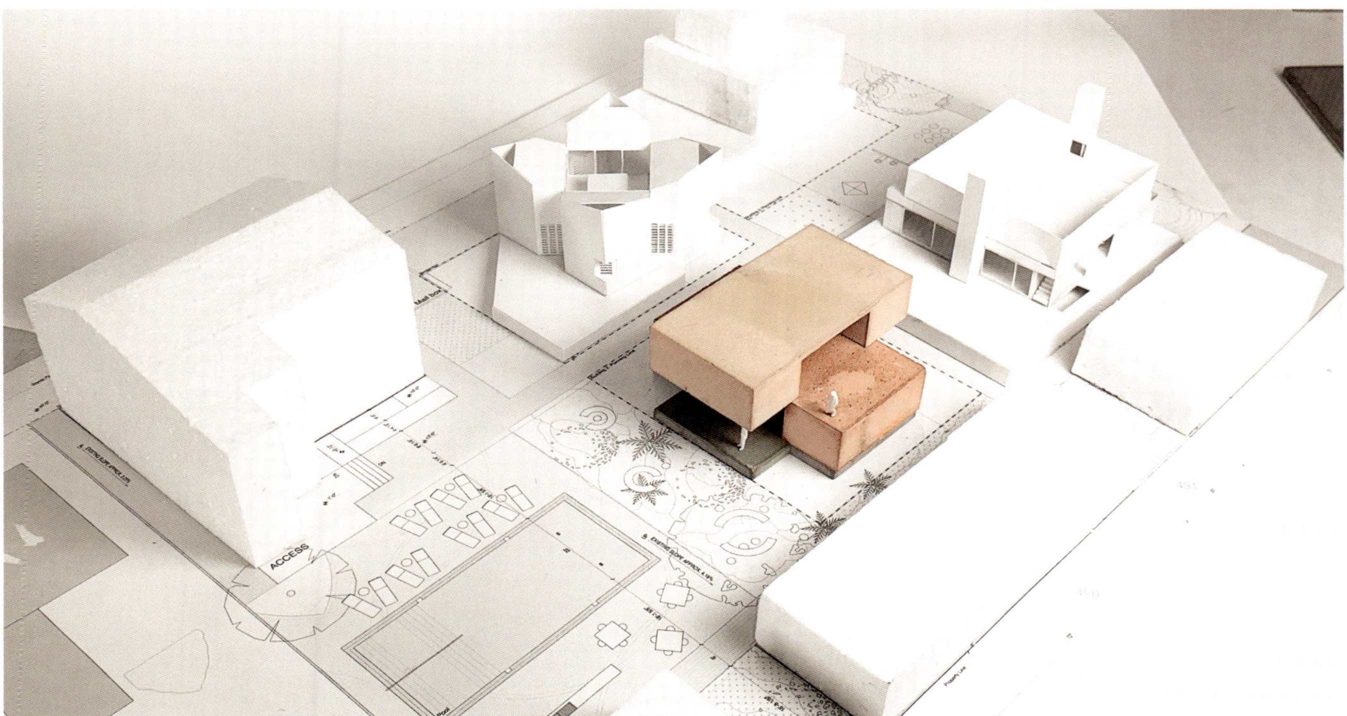
ACCESS

Above and Opposite: Olive West South

Opposite: Olive West South; Above and right: Olive West South interior

Above and opposite: Olive West South interior

KLOSTER MARIA FRIEDENSHORT

On a former secret Stasi site, in the forest, near the town of Neuzelle, Germany, Tatiana Bilbao ESTUDIO, in collaboration with MAIO Architects (Spain) and DOGMA Architects (Belgium), is designing the first new monastery for the Cistercian Order in Brandenburg since the Middle Ages.

The essential question for the design team was to ask: "What should a twenty-first century Cisterican monastery be like?" In several construction phases, a contemporary translation of the ideal Cistercian plan is created. Starting from the main cloister of the monastery, a geometric system of *ad quadratum* defines the proportions and positions of the various courtyard, buildings, and rooms of the complex. The notion of the square cloister, the center, and intersection of the axes, is increasingly broken up into the subsequential buildings. The precinct respects the essential principles of Cistercian architecture: unity, modesty, and liturgy.

The monastery is a rich type in that it perfectly reflects the lifestyle, the daily rituals, rhythms of prayer, and responsibilities of its inhabitants. Certain rooms are evolutions of 1,000-year-old typologies, loaded with symbolism and intricacies that must be understood in the present day. Symbolic concerns frequently govern the monastery. It is a sacred precinct that must still house the mundane. It contains the complete gradient of privacy, extending from the monk's robe to his cell to the abbey wall. It makes many aspects of daily life communitarian. It is the domestic space par excellence.

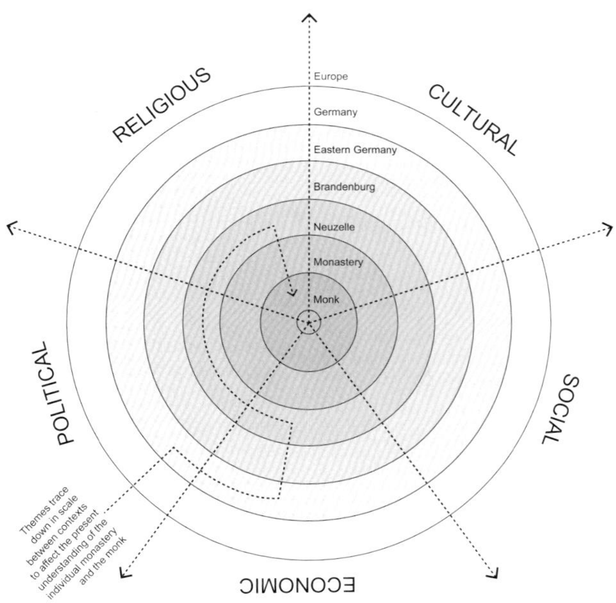

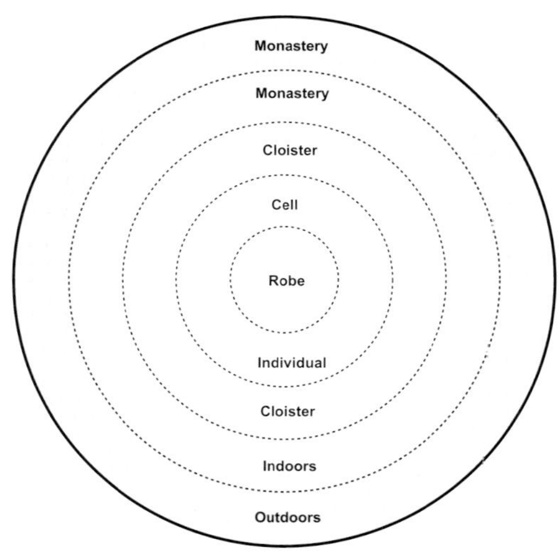

Neuzelle Monastery organziational diagram

Kloster Maria Frieden short concept collage

The proposed unit system starts from the body of a monk and his place in the choir of the church, taking 72 cm. as a starting point (a multiple of the number 12).

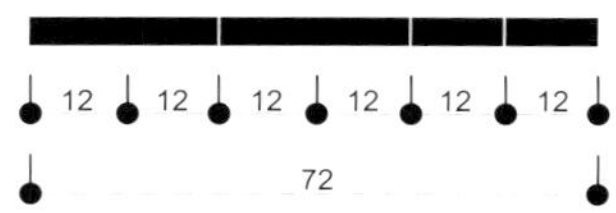

The basis for the design departs from the symbolic number 12, a number referred to completitude (Twelve Apostles, Twelve Tribes of Israel, Twelve Fruits of the Holy Spirit, and twelve thousand furlongs being the dimensions of the Heavenly Jerusalem with twelve jeweled fountains, twelve gates, etc.).

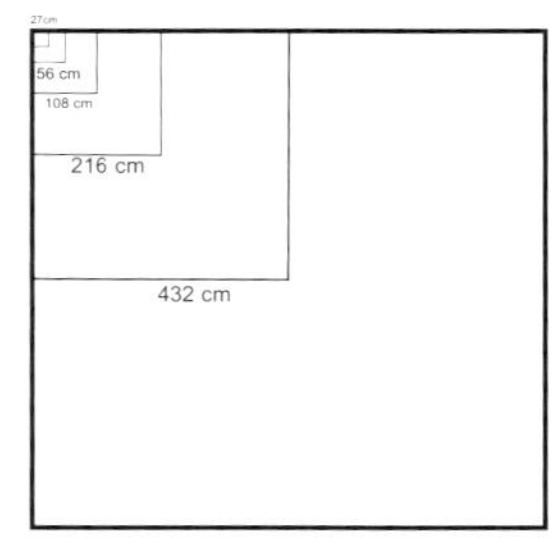

The dimension of the ad quadratum can be divided in proportions 1:2, resulting in the minimum indivisible whole number of the series [27 = 3 x 3 x 3 = (9x3)].

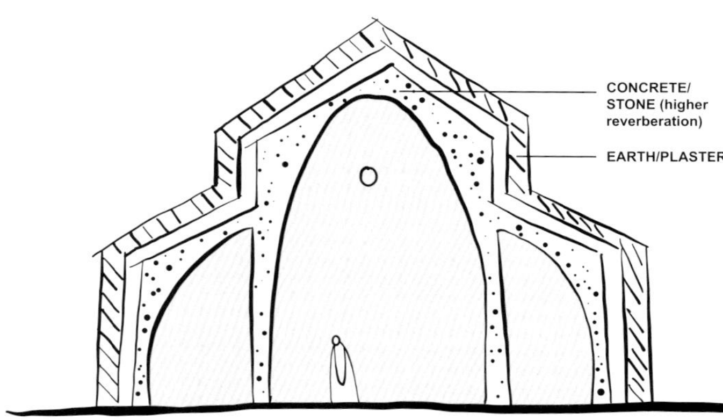

Kloster Maria Friedenshort diagrams

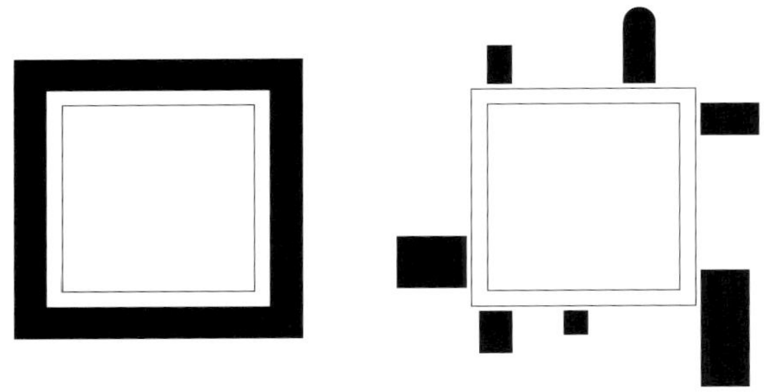

Complete Figures Broken Incomplete

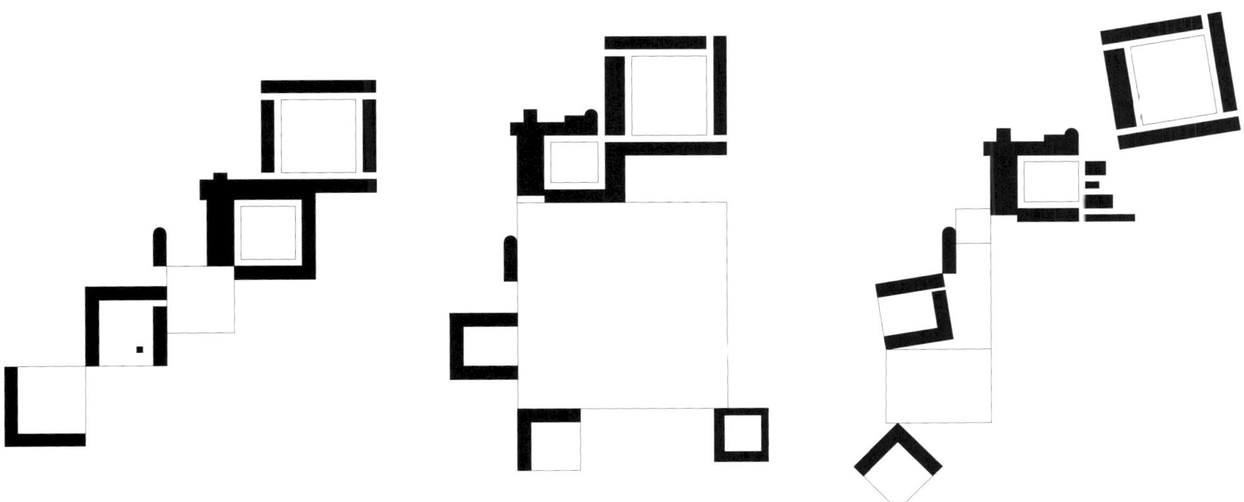

1. Diagonal 2. Lawn 3. Scattered

Kloster Maria Friedenshort diagrams

Kloster Maria Friedenshort concept sketch

Kloster Maria Friedenshort concept model

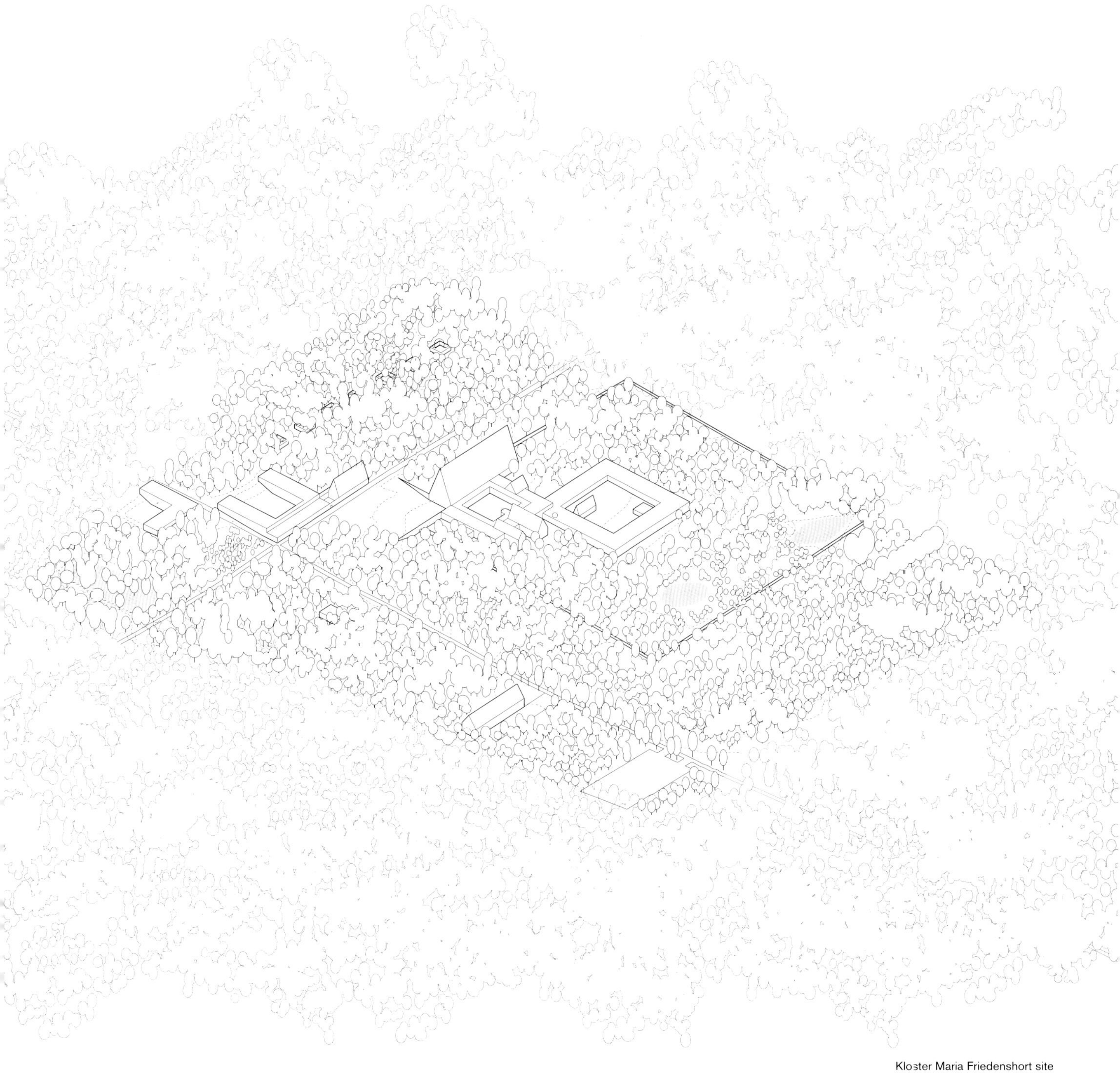

Kloster Maria Friedenshort site

PROJECT CREDITS & DATA

HOUSING +

CHICAGO ARCHITECTURAL BIENNIAL HOUSING
Chicago Cultural Center
Chicago, United States
41°53'01.5"N
87°37'29.9"W
Oct 2015 - Jan 2016

CREDITS
Principal: Tatiana Bilbao
Partners: David Vaner, Catia Bilbao
Office Manager: Juan Pablo Benlliure
Communication Manager: Gabriela Álvarez. Project Manager: Alba Cortés Design Team: Valentina Marchetti, Enrique Silva, Sonia Castañón, Abelardo Bravo, Alejandro Campos, Karen Díaz de León
Models: Rodolfo Díaz. Photos: Enrique Macias
Exhibition Photos: Alejandro Spamer

CHIAPAS HOUSING PROTOTYPE
San Cristobal, Chiapas, México
16°44'31.2"N
92°37'45.6"W
2013 – 2014
52 m2 (2 units)
Built

CREDITS
Principal: Tatiana Bilbao
Partner: Catia Bilbao
Office Manager: Juan Pablo Benlliure. Project Manager: Alba Cortés. Design Team: Enrique Silva, Sonia Castañon, Valentina Marchetti, Abelardo Bravo, Alejandro Campos, Karen Díaz de León
Photos: Tatiana Bilbao ESTUDIO

ACUÑA HOUSING PROTOTYPE
Acuña, Coahuila, México.
29°17'56.5"N
100°57'39.5"W
52 m2 (16 units)
2015
Built

CREDITS
Principal: Tatiana Bilbao
Partner: Catia Bilbao
Office Manager: Juan Pablo Benlliure. Project Manager: Mariano Castillo. Design Team: Abelardo Bravo, Yarla Rangel, Alba Cortés, Enrique Silva, Sonia Castañón, Meghan Mcallister, Kara Biczkowski, Julcsi Fruto.
Client: State of Coahuila
Project promoter: INFONAVIT
Photos: Jaime Navarro, Iwan Baan

ACUÑA MASTEPLAN
Acuña, Coahuila, México.
29°17'56.5"N
100°57'39.5"W
Masterplan: 27, 021 m2
Housing: 52 m2 (16 units)
2015
Built

CREDITS
Principal: Tatiana Bilbao
Partner: Catia Bilbao
Office Manager: Juan Pablo Benlliure. Project Manager: Mariano Castillo. Design Team: Abelardo Bravo, Yarla Rangel, Alba Cortés, Enrique Silva, Sonia Castañón, Meghan Mcallister, Kara Biczkowski, Julcsi Fruto.
Client: State of Coahuila
Project Promoter: INFONAVIT
Photos: Jaime Navarro, Iwan Baan

LYON LA CONFLUENCE, Ilot A3

La Confluence, Lyon, France
45°44'30.2"N
4°49'14.9"E
13,320 m^2 - 3 buildings
2013 – 2017
Built
Certificate: RT 2012 niveau Effinergie +

Bâtiment 3
2,560 m2

Bâtiment 7
3,360 m2

Bâtiment 8
7,400 m2

CREDITS
Principal: Tatiana Bilbao
Partners: David Vaner, Catia Bilbao
Office Manager: Juan Pablo Benlliure. Project Manager: Alessia Shoor. Design Team: Paola Toriz, Moisés Alcántara, Valentina Marchetti, Sofía Betancur, Alba Cortés, Sonia Castañón, Julieta Sobral, Vania Torres, Sergio Torres, Alec Perkins, Yolanda de Rueda, Abelardo Bravo, Andrea Lafarga, Karen Díaz de León. Renders and 3D: Moíses Alcantara, Sofia Betancur, Sonia Castañon, Valentina Marchetti. Model Team Manager: Isaac Monterrosa. Model Team: Victor Castañeda, Veronica Nazar, Eliana Lopez, Ángela Silva, Patricia Morales
Masterplan: Herzog & De Meuron
Client: Icade Promotion
Local Architect: AFAA
Structural Design and Engineering: CETIS Structure
Costs: ILIADE
Sustainability: ARCOBA, Etamine
Photos: Jonathan Letobloun, Iwan Baan

OLIVE WEST

St. Louis, Missouri, USA
38° 38' 24.1" N
90° 14' 13.2" W
20,000 m2
2018 – 2019
Masterplan

CREDITS
Principal: Tatiana Bilbao
Partners: Catia Bilbao, Juan Pablo Benlliure
Project Director: Udayan Mazumdar, Mariano Castillo. Project Manager: Sofía Betancur, Simona Solorzanc
Design Team: Emma Woodward, Alan Bigelow, Dylan Impinck.
Model Team Manager: Isaac Monterrosa. Model Team: Victor Castañeda, Io Plouin, Verónica Nazar, Emerson Carmona
Collaboration: Michael Benz Architecture, PRODUCTORA, MOS Architects, Estudio Macías Peredo, Mitchell Wall Architecture & Design
Photo of Model: Rodrigo Chapa

KLOSTER MARIA FRIEDENSHORT

Neuzelle, Brandenburg, Germany
52°05'25.0"N
14°39'15.7"E
6000 m2
2017 - 2020
Project

CREDITS
Principal: Tatiana Bilbao.
Partners: Catia Bilbao, Juan Pablo Benlliure
Collaborators: DOGMA, MAIO
Tatiana Bilbao ESTUDIO. Project Director: Udayan Mazumdar, Alba Cortés. Project Manager: Simona Solorzano. Design Team: Francisco Lozano, Dylan Impink.

Hunter's Point Substation collage

BIOGRAPHIES

BENJAMIN WILKE (1975–2023) was a senior lecturer at the Knowlton School at The Ohio State University, where he taught architectural design studios and other courses. As series editor of the Source Books in Architecture series from 2015 to 2023, he produced publications on the work of Stan Allen, Preston Scott Cohen, Neil Denari, Ryue Nishizawa/SANAA, Rem Koolhaas/OMA + AMO, and Johnston Marklee.

DEBORAH BERKE, FAIA, is the J.M. Hoppin Professor and dean of the Yale School of Architecture. She is also the founding principal of TenBerke, a New York City based architectural firm.

KAY BEA JONES is a professor emerita at the Ohio State University Knowlton School of Architecture. She is the author of *Suspending Modernity: the Architecture of Franco Albini* and coeditor of the *Routledge Companion to Italian Fascist Architecture: Legacy and Reception.*

TATIANA BILBAO founded her eponymous studio in 2004 with the objective of integrating social values, collaboration, and sensitivity into architecture. The studio's work often intersects with research, enabling the design of solutions for diverse circumstances, including reconstruction, and crisis scenarios. Before establishing her firm, Bilbao served as an advisor in the Ministry of Development and Housing of the Government of the Federal District of Mexico City. During this time, she was involved in the General Development Directorate of the Advisory Council for Urban Development in the city.

Bilbao holds a recurring teaching position at Yale University School of Architecture and has also taught at prestigious institutions such as Harvard University GSD, the Architectural Association in London, Columbia University GSAPP, Rice University, the University of Andrés Bello in Chile, and the Peter Behrens School of Arts at HS Dusseldorf in Germany. Her work has been published in renowned publications such as the *New York Times*, *A + U,* and *Domus*, among others.

Bilbao has received several notable recognitions throughout her career. She won the Kunstpreis Berlin in 2012; the Emerging Voice by the Architecture League of New York in 2010; the Global Award for Sustainable Architecture Prize by the LOCUS Foundation in 2014; the Impact Award Honorees for the Architizer A+ Awards in 2017; the Marcus Prize in 2019 and the Tau Sigma Delta Gold Medal in 2020; the Honorary Fellow of the Royal Architectural Institute of Canada (RAIC); the Richard Neutra Award in 2022; and most recently, the AW Architect of the Year 2022.

JUAN PABLO BENLLIURE is a partner and director of operations at Tatiana Bilbao ESTUDIO, responsible for overseeing the daily operations and making strategic decisions for the office. As the chief operating officer (COO), he serves as the liaison between the general director, finance director, and various architecture workshops. His role includes coordination and control of design, architecture and engineering management, planning and scheduling, and cost control.

With sixteen years of professional experience, Juan Pablo has collaborated on various projects in urban design, architectural design, and interior design. He joined Tatiana Bilbao ESTUDIO in 2008, and has worked in different positions and on various phases of projects. Some of the notable projects he has been involved in include Jardín Botánico Culiacán, Edificio BioInnova, Ecole Maternelle, Casa Ventura, Los Terrenos, Lyon La Confluence, Torres Veracruz, Territorio de Gigantes, Vivienda Popular, Staterra, Centro de Arte Contemporáneo Arévalo, Torre Guatemala, Parque Mazatlán, Edificio Poniente UDEM, Research Center of Sea of Cortez, Silica, Hunters Point, San Francisco, and Olive West in St. Louis, among others.

Juan Pablo completed his studies at the Facultad de Arquitectura of the Universidad Nacional Autónoma de México (UNAM) from 2002 to 2007, where he received a Mention of Honor for his academic achievements.

CATIA BILBAO joined Tatiana Bilbao ESTUDIO in 2009 as the finance director and partner. In her role as chief financial officer (CFO), Catia oversees the financial operations and development of the studio. She is responsible for financial planning, optimizing cash flow, resource management, and executing strategic priorities. She works closely with the management team in matters related to budget management, cost-benefit analysis, and forecasting needs for projects and the organization as a whole. Prior to joining the studio, Catia gained experience working as a financial analyst in the banking system and housing sector. She also worked as a cost and profitability manager for an airline.

Catia completed her bachelor of science in economics at the Instituto Tecnológico Autónomo de México (ITAM) from 1994 to 1999. She later pursued a master of science in operational research at the London School of Economics and Political Science (LSE) from 2003 to 2004.

MARIANO CASTILLO is a partner and project manager at Tatiana Bilbao ESTUDIO. He has an MBA with a specialization in project management and has gained work experience in international offices in Spain and Denmark. Additionally, Mariano currently holds a teaching position at the Universidad Iberoamericana CDMX.

Within Tatiana Bilbao ESTUDIO, Mariano brings valuable knowledge regarding best practices and project management across a wide range of building typologies, including social housing, residential housing, high-density housing, mixed-use buildings, public facilities, and urban design.

Mariano is currently overseeing projects in Mexico, France, and the USA. Some of the notable projects he has led at the office include ESTOA in Monterrey, Port de Montreuil in Paris, and the Boyle Heights master plan.

Mariano received his degree in architecture at the University of the Americas Puebla in Mexico from 2002 to 2008. He studied at The Polytechnic University of Valencia in Spain from 2004 to 2005. He earned an MBA with Magna Cum Laude distinction and a graduate specialization in project management from the University of the Americas Puebla, between 2018 and 2020.

ALBA CORTÉS is a partner and project director at Tatiana Bilbao ESTUDIO. She is responsible for overseeing strategic projects and research within the office. With experience in international offices based in Spain, the United States, and Mexico, Alba has accumulated thirteen years of professional experience.

Throughout her career, Alba has contributed to the design, administration, and execution of various projects of different scales, including housing, urban plans, theaters, museums, and cultural centers. Some notable projects she has been involved in are The Architect's Studio and Tatiana Bilbao Study at the Louisiana Museum of Modern Art, the Chicago Architecture Biennial in 2015, the Mazatlan Aquarium, the Hunterspoint Masterplan in San Francisco, and Collegium: Art Production and Research in Arévalo, Spain, among others.

Alba has also been actively engaged in research projects related to low-cost housing and social participation. Examples of such projects include the Ocoyoacac Minimum Housing, Regional Single Family Housing, Sustainable Housing in Chiapas, and Acuña Sustainable Housing in Mexico. In collaboration with Tatiana Bilbao ESTUDIO, Alba has been awarded the Graham Foundation scholarship twice.

Alba studied at ETSAM (Escuela Técnica Superior de Madrid) at the Universidad Politécnica de Madrid from 2001 to 2009.

SOLEDAD RODRIGUEZ is a partner and holds the role of project execution and construction administration director at Tatiana Bilbao ESTUDIO. With ten years of professional experience, Soledad has been involved in the design, execution, and administration of projects of various scales, including private homes, housing complexes, towers, hotels, cultural centers, and urban and landscape plans. Some notable projects she has worked on include Research Center of Sea of Cortez, UDEM, Parque Central Mazatlán, Casa Tortugas in Nayarit, Casa Durango in Mexico City, and the reconstruction of houses affected by the 2017 earthquake, among others. Having lived and worked in both Spain and Mexico, Soledad brings extensive technical knowledge in the field of architecture to the team.

From 2003 to 2009, Soledad Rodriguez studied technical architecture at the Escuela Politécnica Superior de Burgos. In 2011, she attended the ETSAM (Escuela Técnica Superior de Arquitectura) for further studies in architecture. She also holds a Master's degree in design and interior architecture (MDAI).

PHOTO / IMAGE CREDITS

All reasonable efforts have been made to trace the copyright holders of the visual material reproduced in this book. The publisher and the Knowlton School apologize to anyone who has not been reached. Errors and omissions should be brought to our attention and will be corrected in future editions. All visual content courtesy of Tatiana Bilbao ESTUDIO, except as follows:

Photos by Rodrigo Chapa: 6–7, p33 (top), 23 (bottom left), 33 (top), 103 (bottom), back cover
Photos by Phil Arnold: 13, 58
Photo by Steve Hall : 15 © Steve Hall
Photo by Kate Shanasy:p16
Photos by Jaime Navarro: 23 (top left), 24 (top), 30 (bottom), 73 (bottom), 90, 93 (bottom), 96–97
Photo by José Hevia: 30 (top)
Photos by Iwan Baan: 35 (top and bottom), 72 (top and bottom), 73 (top), 93 (top), 107
Photos by Percibald Garcia: 36, 64–65
Photo by Marlene Hildebrandt: 40
Photo by Rory Gardiner: 44
Photos by Rafeal Gamo: 45 (left and right)
Photo by Enrique Macias Martinez: 61
Photos by Jonathan Letoublon: 106, 108 (top and bottom), 109 (top and bottom), 113 (top and bottom), 117 (top and bottom), 121
Photo by Maxime Delvaux: 125
Photos by Onnis Luque: 133 (bottom), 144 (top)
Photos by Kay Bea Jones: 143, 145 (top and bottom)
Photos by Tatiana Bilbao: 144 (bottom left and bottom right), 147

Tatiana Bilbao ESTUDIO Publication Project Team
Principal: Tatiana Bilbao
Partners: Catia Bilbao, Juan Pablo Benlliure, Alba Cortés, Mariano Castillo, Soledad Rodríguez. Director of Research and Strategic Projects: Alba Cortés.
Project Management: Sebastián Vizcaíno, Isaac Solis Rosas.
Press and Communication Team: Gabriela Montoya, Sofía Martínez.

ACKNOWLEDGMENTS

This publication would not be possible without the generosity and efforts of a number of people. Thanks to everyone at Tatiana Bilbao ESTUDIO. Isaac Solis Rosas, Sebastian Vizcaino, Sofia Martinez, and Gabriela Montoya deserve special thanks, as their communication and efforts with everything related to this publication quite literally made it possible.

A particular thank you to Tatiana Bilbao for her hospitality, kindness, and commitment to this publication amidst a very busy schedule.

Thank you to Deborah Berke and Kay Bea Jones, whose contributions to this publication are welcome perspectives on the work of Tatiana Bilbao ESTUDIO.

At the Knowlton School, thank you to Dorothee Imbert and Phu Hoang, who continue to be supportive of the *Source Books in Architecture* series. Thank you to Jaimie Mollison, Carla Sharon, Phil Arnold, and the whole of the Knowlton School administrative team for their assistance with this and every publication.

As always, thanks to Gordon Goff and Jake Anderson at ORO/AR+D for their guidance, expertise, and professionalism.

Finally, Andi Moore's assistance and hard work has been essential to the success of this book. Her ability to balance levity and attention to detail has made working on this project that much more enjoyable. You made my job easier. Thank you, Andi.

In Memoriam
Benjamin Wilke, longtime editor of the Source Books in Architecture series, died on 13 November 2023, at the age of 48, just as this book was nearing completion. Ben was a loving father to his son, Leo, and a gifted designer, a valued colleague, and a beloved teacher at the Knowlton School.

We dedicate this book to his memory.